Chain of Foals
-from farm to finish line

Susan K. Walsh

Color Edition

Chain of Foals
-from farm to finish line

Susan K. Walsh

Color Edition

PEAR TREE PUBLISHING

Chain of Foals
-from farm to finish line

Copyright © 2020 by Susan K. Walsh

No part of this book may be reproduced in any form or by electronic or mechanical means including information storage and retrieval systems without permission in writing from the author, except in the case of brief quotations used in reviews.

Published by Pear Tree Publishing
www.PearTreePublishing.net

First Color Edition

Published in the United States of America

Walsh, Susan K.
    Chain of Foals / by Susan K. Walsh – 1st Ed.
    ISBN 978-1-62502-032-1
    Library of Congress Control Number: 2019915493

    1. Horse Breeding - Author. 2. Horse Racing – New England 3. Horse Racing – Suffolk Downs 4. Horse Racing – History
    I. Title II. North Andover, MA – History III. Equine Farming

Cover & Book Design by Susan K. Walsh & Christopher P. Obert
Cover photos courtesy of Susan and Jim Walsh
4 5 6 7 8 9 10

Also by Susan K. Walsh
Edgewood, an Old Farm in the New Millennium
(2011) ISBN 978-0-9821983-1-5

To Jim: the other part of the entry.

TABLE OF CONTENTS

Preface - - - - - - 9

PART I

Sin Mill (Millie) - - - - - 15
Petrifier (Pete) - - - - - 41
He's Dansin (Dansin) - - - - 61
Duly Royal (Duly) & Agatha C. (Aggie) - 91
Penance (The Rodent) - - - - 119
Sunny Reign (Reign) - - - - 125
Sunny Crime (O2B) - - - - 145
Sunny Stand (Macho) - - - - 155
Due To Land (Teeny) - - - - 173
Due To Shine (Shine) - - - - 195
Duly's Dancer (Timmy) & Regan's Ridge (Johnny) 205
Sundance Land (Herbie) - - - - 227
Party Pants (Betty) - - - - - 233

PART II

After the Wire - - - - - 243
The Cast of Characters - - - - 248
The Winner's Circle - - - - 253
The Dope on Drugs - - - - 255
Some Random Conclusions - - - 259

EPILOGUE

Chain of Foals - - - - - 265

PREFACE

They run through my dreams, all the foals I've delivered, galloping over the fields of my memory. They whirl past, my own merry-go-round: chestnut, bay, blood bay, near-black ….bottle-brush tails flagging, Mohawk manes tossing in the wind, impossibly long, thin legs drumming heartbeats on the grass. I watch them run, and remember the moment of their births, each one different; and see their careers foretold in the look of an eye, the intent of their stride. My chain of foals.

This all came about because of Anticipation. Not the abstract noun anticipation, but Anticipation the large white pony. She was a boarder at the farm where we lived; and one day in spring when I drove up to the barn, I saw two little girls clinging desperately to her in the road as she spun around, perilously close to breaking loose. She was for sale, I knew, and hadn't been out of her stall in weeks. This was one of those spring days in New England when the sun is shining, but the wind is cold and brutal, and she was wild with the excitement of being outside. The two girls were bravely struggling to hang on, but it looked like a losing battle.

When I approached them, the older of the two, Trina, told me they'd bought her and were going to walk her home. Home? Yes, to Trina's family farm, which was "only" a few miles away. I told them to put her back in her stall until I could get my trailer, and I'd drive them. It didn't take long to hitch up the trailer, and soon we were all on the way. The pony was fine in the trailer, and the two girls were thrilled.

When we drove up to Trina's house, a stunning horse came running up to the fence to watch the arrival of the newcomer. When I asked, Trina said "That's my father's mare," and dashed off with her excited friend and her new pony. I went back home and went on with my life.

Late that fall, I was visiting John Roche at his farm, three miles away. He and his daughter, Cathy, had a barn and a small training track, and they'd take layups from the racetrack. John often came to our farm in his old truck to buy hay and we'd become friends. A few years before, I'd even taken one of his old racehorses as a project. He was a wealth of knowledge about anything concerning horses and their various injuries, and I'd often stop in to see him if I was in the area. That day, we were in their barn looking at the horses, and he casually mentioned, "Oh, Frank Dinardi's got one of his mares for sale." Not only was it the handsome mare who'd caught my eye that spring, but she was in foal.

A life-changing moment! I'd tried to get my husband Jim more interested in horses. I'd tried getting him to go to shows with me ("too boring!"), tried getting him to ride ("too boring and painful!") and had finally had some success in getting him to the races at nearby Rockingham Park. When I bought him Andy Beyer's book, *Picking Winners*, he was finally hooked by the challenge of handicapping. Now, I realized in a blinding flash that here was a chance to ramp up his interest: we could raise our own racehorse!

I had had a little experience in horse raising: I'd owned a pony that I'd bred myself (although I'd missed the actual foaling), the farm we lived on now bred Welsh ponies, and Woody, the manager, had decades of experience in raising horses. I'd overseen the birth and childhood of one of my friend's mares, also a Thoroughbred. We now lived on-site in a little house out back; and being a teacher, I had a long summer vacation every year. We were also young enough to think we could do this. I had always had a love of racing: my own horse was an ex-race horse, and I still had scrapbooks from my childhood full of old articles from Sports Illustrated about horse racing. I could work at Rockingham during my summer vacation and learn more about the racing end of this; it would be fun – right? So, late that fall, I once again hitched up my trailer and drove to Dinardi's farm, and just before Christmas brought home Tenny Peche, heavily in foal.

Three month old Millie.

CHAIN OF FOALS

PART I

Sin Mill (Millie)

Tenny settled in quickly at the farm. My wonderful old gelding, Majorca, turned out to be a perfect companion, so the two of them had lots of pasture time. It was a fairly easy winter: snow, yes, but lots of sunny days. I had plenty of time to plan for the foal, too, reading up on the foaling process and talking with Woody. He actually confessed that even though they'd had lots of foals by then, most of the time, he missed the actual births. The Welsh pony mares were cagey about it: he'd check on them, then go make coffee, and come back and find a little foal up and nursing.

As Tenny's foaling date approached, I started scrutinizing her udder, looking for the telltale signs of imminent birth. It seemed like she was in an eternal holding pattern, but finally, in mid-April, her udder slowly began to fill. I started doing night checks, and unscrewed the light in her stall to avoid disturbing her when I'd walk in. We had her settled into what Woody called the stud barn: a small building, almost a lean-to design, with six stalls in a row and an aisle running along their front.

There was a door at one end, and a door at the far end which opened to the manure pile. There were also two Dutch doors that opened into two fairly good sized paddocks, facing south, and windows running along that whole side – so during the winter, with the sun streaming in, it was cozy and warm.

Now, things were starting to change. Tenny's udder at first was puffy, with a groove down the middle, but one day, it was filled to capacity and finally, the much-heralded "waxing up." Now we were getting close! That night, I checked once, then again and by this point, I was getting impatient. In the dead of night, I gave one more check. I slipped in the back door over the manure pile, crept down the aisle, listened to the deep breathing of the horse in the first stall I came to, then peered in at her. She was just standing there in the shadows, and I almost left but I noticed how shiny she looked.

Shiny? I reached over and put a hand on her neck, and it was slick with sweat.

Suddenly, I was not so impatient. My first thought was, "Oh, wait! Let's do this tomorrow!" My second thought was a flash on all the ways this could go very wrong. My third thought was that I was alone here, and the vet was at least an hour away. Stop the world!

There is no "pause" button for a mare in labor, however; and a second after all these thoughts raced through my brain, she went down. We'd bedded the stall in nice fresh straw, and she flopped over on her side, then rolled, then leapt to her feet and to my horror, a single leg in its rubber sack thrust out from under her tail. She flung herself down again, and a wave of panic ran through me. She rolled, stood up, and the leg retreated. Then, down again; and now she lay on her side, groaning. The leg reappeared, with another one a little behind. The mare had a few more contractions, and the legs wobbled forward, then back. I slipped into the stall, took a deep breath, and gingerly took hold of them, then, thinking madly of all that I'd read, when the next contraction came, pulled carefully down toward her hocks and in a rush, out came the two legs, and lying in the groove between them, a foal's head all in her cowl. Another contraction, and the hips followed and suddenly, surfing forward on a wave of briny fluid, a perfect, tiny foal.

This moment of birth was stunning: one minute, me and the mare in the silent night and then, in a flash, another little creature lying in the straw, breathing, moving. This perfect little creature, growing all these months hidden away in her own dark inland sea, then, in a rush, diving out of her watery world into mine. It was a profound moment for me, stunning; one I never tired of.

I may have been elated, but Tenny was tired. She lay back in the deep straw, breathing slowly, eyes closed, but then the foal started struggling to rid herself of her rubbery sack, and her tiny legs bumped into the mare's. Tenny lifted her head, irritated, then saw the foal, and her eyes grew wide. At that moment, the foal made a tiny bleating sound, and Tenny, eyes growing even wider, answered her with a deep, throaty nicker I'd never heard her make before. I could see in her eyes the realization that this little creature was hers. She reached forward, smelled the foal, and leaped to her feet, hovering over her, nickering again, nudging and licking. Another moment I'd never tire of seeing: the little bleat, the realization dawning in the mare's eyes, the answering call.

We were very lucky in our initial foray into Thoroughbred breeding. This foal was healthy and the birth was fairly routine. She struggled around, standing, wobbling, falling down, bumping into the mare … and Tenny hovered protectively. For what seemed hours, but was probably twenty minutes, she'd stagger toward Tenny, bump into her udder, then stagger right past. I stood next to her and steadied her, and eventually, she figured things out. Tenny, with a few preliminary squeals, acquiesced, and stood patiently while she nursed. I ran home to get Jim, and the two of us stood in the aisle watching, marveling at how perfect this foal was. I had iodine ready, and a paper cup and I was able to soak her navel with only a few misses. Finally, she'd nursed to satiety, and she and Tenny settled down. I left the aisle lights on, and Jim and I (and our faithful dog, of course) went back to the house to rest.

In the morning, our wonderful vet, Bob Orcutt, and his assistant, Pat Tataronis, stopped in to examine mother and daughter. When they'd pronounced both healthy, we decided it was time to introduce the foal to the world. Once again, we were lucky: it was April 23, and a sunny, mild day. Their stall was right across from one of the doors to the paddock, so with very little effort, we got them out the door, across the aisle, and into the sunshine. Tenny got a little panicky when Jim started leading her out, spinning around and calling for her foal, but I shuffled along with the baby right behind her. It was only a few steps from stall to paddock, too; and when they got out, Tenny immediately set off at an animated trot, her foal right behind her. This caused a sensation, of course; the other horses in the barn whinnied; horses across the road in the pasture whinnied and soon we had a crowd of people lining the fences. The day was so nice that we were able to leave them out until dusk; and the paddock footing was perfectly dry, with grass just starting to green up. When we wanted to put them in, Tenny got nervous again when we grabbed her, but our dog with his wonderful Border

Collie genes helped us scoop the foal up right behind her and make those few steps from the pasture into the stall again.

Jim and I were guilty of the same excesses as new parents of children: we have more photographs of this foal than all the others combined. We borrowed a movie camera, and somewhere in our treasures there are a few dusty super 8 films of the mare and foal racing around. We started a scrapbook, naturally; and a daily written journal. I still have the scrapbook. It's enormous, of course. We have a smaller one for our second foal, and a folder for the third foal, and after that, just envelopes with pictures crammed in out of order. We went from spring to summer in the euphoria of having a beautiful little foal. She was bright chestnut, with a mane that sprang straight up from her arched neck; and a blaze that slanted fetchingly off the side of her nose. Beautiful, liquid foal eyes, bright red bottle-brush foal tail: the whole package. She was also amazingly vivacious, seeming to be in motion constantly, quick on her feet, darting here and there around the paddock, bucking, rearing. We were smitten.

When she was two weeks old, we decided it was time to slip on a tiny little foal halter; so one day when we were about to turn them out, I stood beside her with the little halter in hand, but she wanted no part of it! We had commented frequently on her agility, and she put it all to use, ducking away, rearing, striking at me with her tiny hooves, twisting, ricocheting all over me, her mother, Jim. This was not going to work, so I went to Plan B: enlisted the services of Ken Brown, the strong, silent man who had helped Woody with innumerable foals in the past. He just walked into the stall, put his right arm around her chest and his left arm around her rear, and held her motionless while I put the halter over her nose.

RESOLVED: We will now halter all our foals the day after they're born.

Well, our plan was to have a foal, and now we did. What we hadn't given much thought to, was that, once you have a foal, you also have a broodmare – and broodmares are supposed to brood! All the people we knew who were breeders bombarded us with suggestions about who to breed her back to, and being the newcomers, we acquiesced and made arrangements to breed Tenny to a stallion just over the New Hampshire border. Five weeks after she was born, our foal had her first trailer ride. I carefully put a bale of hay next to the exit door, so she couldn't accidentally open it; removed the center partition, and loaded them up. Tenny walked right in, and the foal followed right afterward. Off we went for her appointment with destiny, we thought.

The mare and foal were only gone eleven days, and we fretted the whole time. We couldn't wait to retrieve them, and they seemed fine. Tenny had managed to acquire a little fungus on her muzzle, but the foal was in good shape. They were returning alone, though: the breeding didn't take. Once we thought about it, we realized this was a blessing. We had to pay board per stall; now, we paid for two, my gelding and the mare, but in the fall, when the foal was weaned, it would be three. If Tenny had another foal, the next fall would be four, and so on all before our wonder foal even had a chance to earn her living. For our do-it-yourself style and our limited budget, breeding back would quickly overwhelm us.

RESOLVED: Don't breed back. Give the mare (and us!) a year to recover after she foals.

Now that we had a healthy foal, she needed to be registered with the Jockey Club. We took pictures of her – front, back, both sides – and filled in the form describing all her markings. Then, the name! Jim was our official namer, and after tossing around several possibilities, we put down three choices. This daughter of Millstone, out of Tenny Peche ("Peche" being French for "sin"), became in the Jockey Club registry, Sin Mill. In our daily lives, Millie.

As spring turned into summer, we had a blissful period of wonderful weather and trouble-free foal-keeping. When she was three weeks old, Woody had us move her back to the big barn, so she could now go out into a big pasture with her mother for significant periods, and this enabled her to stretch her little legs running up and down the gentle hill. When she was just born, she had very long pasterns, and the first day, her ankles seemed to touch the ground. Running around strengthened them in no time. She grew considerably, started shedding her foal coat, and gained some pretty impressive muscles. Friends of ours who were breeders came to see her, and they all praised her. She really did start to look like a winner. There wasn't much more for us to do at this point except turn her out in the morning and bring her in at night, making sure she had access to fresh clean water. Tenny was mellowed out by her motherhood, too and was content to graze quietly while her baby tore up the pasture running and bucking. When they were in the barn, my gelding Majorca was in the next stall, and there was a small hole in the wall that he and Millie gnawed on and enlarged. Soon, they were fast friends.

In June, the school year came to a close, and I was free for the summer. Time for me to follow through on the other half of this scheme: learning more about the race track. One of the people who came by to look at the foal was a horse owner, and he told me his trainer, Jack, was looking for help, so I drove to Rockingham one morning, looked him up, and within minutes was an official hot walker! Latin Teacher to Hot Walker in one day.

Jack had six horses and two grooms, Maryann Bogochow and Leesa Lavigne, one of which, Maryann, was learning to gallop horses. My job as hot walker would be to cool out the six when they came back from the track. Well, how hard could that be, right?

As it turns out, working for Jack was a great introduction to the backside. He only had six horses, but he'd been doing this for quite a while, and he had a method for everything, and a reason behind his method. He also may have thought that I, being the wife of a lawyer, might be a potential owner; so he was very kind to me, and very patient. I bombarded him with questions constantly, and he always had the answers. To this day, many of the little things I do with my horses follow the Jack school of training. From the way I put snaps on screw eyes, to the way I rake the aisle, all these are little things I learned that first summer that I still do today.

The first thing I learned was how much there was to learn. Yes, my wonderful gelding Majorca was a former racehorse, but that was long ago; and dealing with horses at the track in training was a completely different matter. The very first horse I walked, on the very first day, almost dragged me off my feet. I had to learn how to thread the shank through the halter, how to hold the shank in my hand, what to watch for before it happened, how to place myself in relation to the horse I was walking. Each horse walked for half an hour, circling the shedrow and taking sips of water. I had to learn how to oversee that too: how a horse cooled out could tell an observant hot walker a lot about his fitness and comfort level, both of which were crucial to his training. After the first morning, I was exhausted but exhilarated. And the vocabulary! "Knock off" meant "brushing," "rings" was a running martingale. Then there was a two-minute lick, a picket fence, horsing, a ridgling, jacking up the irons, a spider; every day I learned more of the vernacular, and got to know more of the people who populated this unique world. Harry Hicks came over on a pony every day to escort Maryann to the track, Bucky O'Connor rode by the barn many times a day on his way to and from the track, always joking, with a big crow feather sticking out of his helmet. Tim Hill was a new young trainer with a few horses on the backside of us. When Tim won a race with one of his young horses, Jack predicted, prophetically, that he was going to be a good trainer. There was Max Hall, just starting to make his mark as a jock's agent; and of course a steady stream of jockeys looking for mounts in the afternoon.

My days fell into a wonderful rhythm: leave home early as the mare and foal were turned out, work at Jack's barn, walking the six horses; finish up there by eleven; have a quick lunch at the track kitchen; drive home and collapse for a while; bring the mare and foal in; feed them; feed Jim and me; go to bed early, very early! By midsummer, just the simple routine of walking six horses around a shedrow had turned me into the fittest shape of my life. I loved my job; I loved the racetrack in the morning; I loved the camaraderie.

Looking back at this first venture into breeding racehorses, I'm embarrassed at how obsessive we were: typical new parents. We measured Millie every month, took pictures constantly, compared her to famous horses of the past. She was 12.2 at four months; 13.1 at six months. We set up a little foal feeder in the corner of the stall, and when Tenny would zoom over and vacuum up everything before Millie had even thought about it, we started tying Tenny by her feed tub until Millie was finished. Millie was a pretty little thing, but I'm afraid our doting turned her into a princess. She got very tricky when it was time to bring her in. At the end of a long day in the field, often a hot and buggy one, Tenny was always more than ready to come in for the night, coming right to the gate when she saw me walking across the ring to the pasture. Millie would dash over initially, but then, when I put the shank on Tenny and was ready to open the gate, it was "catch me if you can." She'd come up, wheel, dash off, speed by. Every day, it took longer and longer to get her. I even started leading Tenny through the ring by herself, letting Millie follow behind, but then we'd have the same problem when we got to the gate from the ring to the barn. I feared that we'd created a monster.

Millie at six months with Jim.

At six months, it was time to wean. I was very apprehensive, fearing some kind of equine meltdown, but things went fairly well. We brought the two in at the usual time, and then, I simply did a U-turn with Tenny and led her right back out of the stall. Jim stayed with Millie, and I brought Tenny back to the stud barn. All the way over, I felt so guilty, tearing this mare from her beloved foal, but halfway there, Tenny stopped trying to turn around and figured out being alone without this demanding foal wouldn't be so bad, after all. As for Millie, when she realized Tenny had gone, she did have a mini-meltdown, spinning around, whinnying in panic but then the panic turned to pique, and she had a little tantrum. Fortunately, my wonderful gelding Majorca was right in the next stall, where he always was, and he stuck his big nose through the hole they'd worked on. Within a few minutes, he'd calmed her down.

The bond between Majorca and Millie made the weaning easier, too: the next day we put him out in the pasture, then brought her out. She was carrying on, of course, whinnying for her mother, looking all over the place – but when we led her through the gate and let her go, she saw Majorca up the hill, and made a beeline to him. They greeted each other, then both took off running, down the field to the gate, then roaring past us back up the hill; and halfway up, they slowed down and started grazing.

With the weaning behind her, Millie went into a new but comfortable routine: I'd turn her out with Majorca on my way to school, and they'd stay out all day until I came back. Majorca was the perfect babysitter: always solicitous of her, and always alert to any potential problems. One day I drove up to the barn after school just in time to see Majorca trotting up and down the side fence: a dog - a Great Dane, no less - was trying to get into the pasture. Majorca absolutely wouldn't allow that; and Millie, bored, grazed undisturbed a little distance away.

Fall turned to winter. Normally, we don't baby our horses. We turn them out every day all winter, and let them grow nice heavy coats. If the weather is truly awful, or if it's a raging blizzard, they stay in; but most of the time, they get out and socialize. This winter was fairly typical for New England, until mid-January. We had some rain, which turned to serious ice, and the temperature stayed below freezing for two weeks. The ice glazed everything: every road, every path, every field was covered in a solid sheet. So, what to do with a rambunctious yearling? The barn at the farm was huge: a big bank barn, with a wide main aisle, a huge hayloft, and a full cellar whose south side was accessible from the road. It had been built for cows, and there was an inside ramp which led from the main floor down into the cellar. It was low, but at this point, so was Millie. One day I led her down the ramp to the cellar, which was all open, with a dirt floor. She went down very cautiously, but she went; and when we got there and I turned her loose, she ran around, bucking and kicking, just enough to get the pent-up energy released. That worked so well that we did it for the next few days, until the ice outside softened and we could get her out with Majorca again. That worked so well, in fact, that two of the boarders decided to do that with their ponies, running around down there joyfully until they raised so much dust that they couldn't see or breathe. The poor man's indoor ring.

In January, now a yearling, Millie started having issues with her nose: thick discharge which just wouldn't go away. I started taking her temperature, which was not an easy thing to do, and when it rose, called the vet. Dr. Orcutt made many visits over the next month or so, dispensing various medications. Some seemed to help, some didn't but finally, with the return of spring, her nose cleared up. Whatever caused it did little permanent damage, except to our bank account.

That spring, still smitten by our surely-a-champion filly, we decided to give her more exposure. A local series of horse shows had a class for "horse colts," so we decided to take her. First, the trailer. She had long forgotten her trip to New Hampshire with her mother, but now, her surrogate parent Majorca once again proved to be a priceless asset. One evening, I loaded him in, and she followed without hesitation. After a few practices, we were ready!

For the first show, we trailered over early in the morning. The colt class was the first on schedule, so it wouldn't be a long day. Millie followed Majorca into the trailer, and we were off. When we got to the showgrounds, I ran and got my number, then came back and unloaded Millie. Her class was already assembling, so we went right over. She was fairly well behaved, and it wasn't a long ordeal; but Majorca, back in the trailer, was distraught. The whole time we were gone, he whinnied and pawed. For the second show, he was better and after that, we had all had enough. We thought she was the best of the lot, of course; but the young Arabs and Saddlebreds always placed ahead of her. Oh, well, this was just for experience and we knew she was faster than all of them!

That summer, once school was out, I went back to Rockingham to further my education. This year, I moved up from hot walker to groom. My new employer, John Burke, had a barn full of horses and a reputation for getting them to the winner's circle. He ran his shedrow in the traditional way: every four horses had a groom; there were two hot walkers assigned to cool the horses out, clean feedtubs, and be there to assist. He had a foreman, Dick Kelley, who patrolled the shedrow troubleshooting, and a regular exercise rider. John often galloped his horses in the morning, too. He had a white pony, Weasel, and a pony boy, Jay Botty, who was in charge of keeping Weasel fit and happy. I absolutely loved my new job. The grooms were all professional, masters of the trade: Charlie Greer, John Prince, Peewee Valentine…Peewee became my mentor: he showed me little tricks to getting the bandages on perfectly, to rolling them up, to grooming the horses; and entertained me with all kinds of stories of his experiences. Like many other grooms in those days, he considered himself a professional and took real pride in the condition of his horses. The day started early; and most days, if John had a horse running, we were all expected to be there after the races, too. By July, I was fit and also constantly exhausted. By August, I'd become accustomed to the workload. By September, I considered abandoning my teaching job and running away to the circus that was Thoroughbred Racing.

At the end of the Rockingham meet, the Yankee Thoroughbred Breeders held their annual yearling show, and we were ready! John let us use one of his stalls for that morning, so we brought Millie in. The crew at the barn was complimentary: they all agreed she was a good looking filly. I brushed her off, put her chiffney bit in, and proudly led her up to the grandstand. There was a fairly good crowd up there watching. Fillies went first, then colts. She behaved pretty well, and I was so nervous, or maybe beyond nervous, that it all passed in a daze. At the end, she was placed third; I still have the ribbon hanging in the tack room at home.

On November 1, I started to break her. "Break" by my method was hardly dramatic: I just got her used to being tacked up in her stall. Then, when she was used to that, one day I led her up and down the aisle with the tack on, and finally, and very carefully, had Jim hold her while I stood on some hay bales and leaned over her. Then, more carefully, I swung my leg over and eased into the saddle. Much patting. Then, Jim led us back down the aisle, and I got off. Phew!

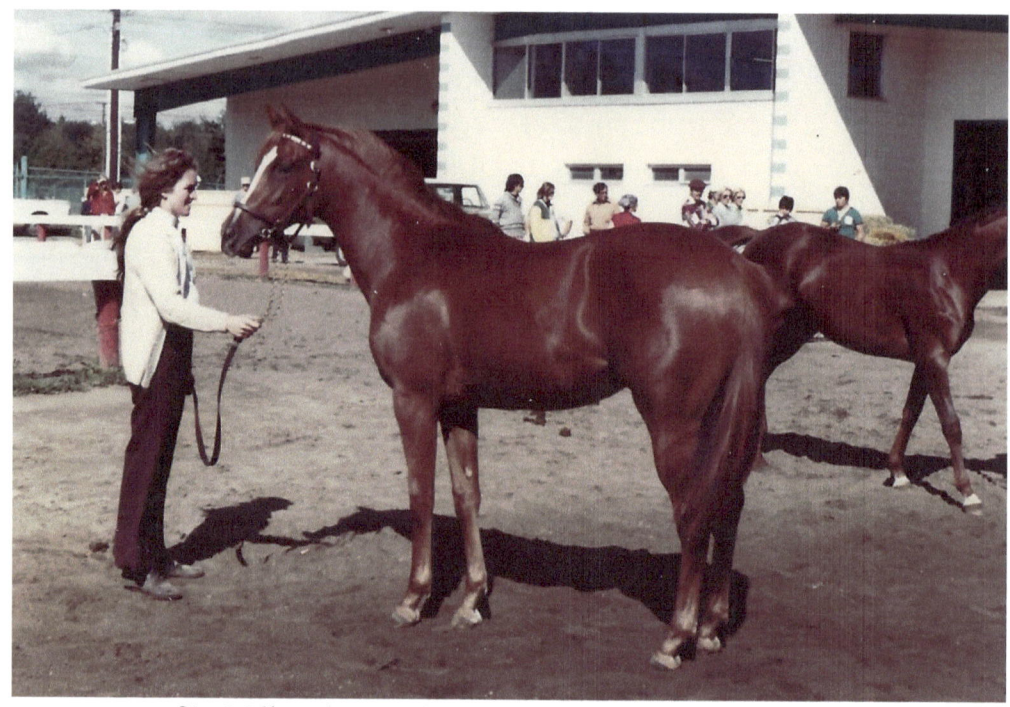

Sin Mill at the Yearling Show at Rockingham, 1977.

For the next few days, we did the same thing: tack up, get on, walk down the aisle maybe a time or two, and then dismount. She was surprisingly amenable to all this, and we read that as still another sign that she was destined for greatness.

Our first attempt at breeding our own race horse was proceeding on course: we now had three stalls at the farm: our broodmare, Marjorca, and Millie - and we could manage the expenses fairly well. Now, we had a nice yearling who'd been to shows, was developing on schedule, and, "outstanding in her field," seemed to us full of potential. We got her papers from the Jockey Club, and there, on the timeless Jockey Club certificate, was her name, Sin Mill and her sire, Millstone, her dam, Tenny Peche. We'd captured her life to date in home movies, on film we had a fat scrapbook to document her progress toward greatness - until November 10!

By November of that year, Rockingham had closed, and I was back teaching school. Jim and I left the farm early in the morning, turning Majorca and Millie out, and I was usually back home by three. Tenny was in foal again, and in the afternoon I'd take her for walks. The farm was beginning to have more and more boarders, so most of the ponies had moved from the big barn to the stud barn and Woody's training barn to make room for the paying customers. The afternoon of November 10, I left school, raced home and when I pulled up to the barn, I could see the pasture where Millie and Majorca should be was empty. My first reaction was annoyance that someone would have taken them in on such a fine fall day, but when I jumped out of the car, Woody met me in the barn door.

"We got the bleeding stopped and Doc and Pat are on their way." My anger turned to horror as I followed Woody into the barn and looked in on our perfect future champion. She was standing right next to the wall, right next to Majorca's nose, a blank expression on her face and a haemostat clamped to her right forearm.

Woody filled me in on the details. He was coming out of the pony barn and looked over to see Majorca and Millie standing next to the gate, which was odd. Then he noticed the red: her whole forearm was mangled and bloody. He and Kenny Brown brought them in, and he called the vet. Apparently, she'd been up on the hill next to the back fence, messing with some of the ponies in the back pasture. The fence there was still the wire/barbed wire they had for the cows; and we think she reared up and somehow hooked her leg on the fence. When she pulled it back, the wire tore right through her skin and muscle. Somehow, she made it back down to the gate and now stood miserably, probably in shock, waiting for the vet.

The vet! Doctor Orcutt and his wonderful assistant, Pat Tataronis! They'd been keeping horses in Essex County healthy and happy for years. Just the sight of their old station wagon pulling into the yard made my anxiety lessen. In they came, and in minutes, led her into the aisle, had Kenny retrieve a floor lamp from his apartment, had me hold the foal, and set to work. They quickly gave her a tranquilizer, and Doctor Orcutt settled down on an old milk crate to assess the damage. The cut had girded her upper arm;

all the skin had slipped down like an old knee sock, bagging around her knee. One muscle of her forearm was almost severed, and the large vein beside it cut. When Dr. Orcutt removed the hemostat, a thin jet of blood shot out. Carefully and deliberately, he began: stemming the blood, stitching the shreds of muscle together. Pat helped, handing him needles, pointing things out ("Wait, what about this piece?"), mopping up blood. Finally, after the torn muscle and vein had been repaired, he grasped the baggy skin and pulled it up over her knee, and sewed it back in place. I breathed a sigh of relief, but Pat said, "Let's see how she can walk," and when she took one step forward, it all fell apart. More blood, more gore. Dr. Orcutt never spoke, just went right back in and with excruciating care, did it all over again. That time, it seemed to hold. Then, the bandaging. He left a wick in for drainage, and encased the whole leg in thick cotton sheets and then bandage. We eased her back to her stall, and Pat fitted her halter with a bib to keep her from ripping the whole thing apart. At last, they drove off, planning to return the next day. Later, Pat told me, "When we drove off, Doc looked at me and said, 'That'll never hold!'"

Well, it did. Jim and I stayed with her all night, running in to bring water to her so she wouldn't have to move; offering her hay when she got restless. At one point, Jim, in despair, said that our whole dream was over when the horse in the next stall, Tenny, snorted as if to say, "Well, I'm over here working on another one!"

She did make it through the night. Pat and Doc returned the next day, teased the wick out a little, reset her bandage, gave us encouragement. The other boarders brought us coffee and goodies, and moved in and out of the barn as quietly as they could. The leg swelled horribly. It puffed up over the top of the bandage like ice cream over a cone. Things did get better, though. After five days, Doc thought the immediate danger was over. The horrible swelling subsided; she seemed more comfortable; we took turns going home for rest. Gradually, I'd ease the wick out, and I'd flush out the hole it left every day. After three weeks, Dr. Orcutt pulled the outside stitches and declared her healed. He said the leg would be swollen for up to a year, until collateral veins formed to replace the big one that had been severed, but she was good to go.

We walked her by hand, up and down the aisle when it was quiet, and then, gradually, outside. Finally, five weeks after the accident, we turned her out in Woody's round pen. It was a glorious winter day: cold, but with bright sun and virtually no wind. I gave her a little tranquilizer beforehand, but in my anxiety, spilled most of it on the floor. She was tranquil for the count of three, and then wildly euphoric; but the snow was great padding, and the other horses by the fence kept her focused. We took pictures, of course.

After three weeks of turnout in the round pen, on another brilliant winter day with a fresh coating of snow, she went out in the pasture with Majorca. He'd kept vigil all this time, standing by the hole between their stalls when they were inside; and standing by the fence when she was turned out. Now, reunited, they raced up the hill and back, plumes of snow in their wake. She seemed perfect!

Her leg was still swollen, of course; not as grotesque as it had been initially, but enough to keep me wrapping it. Every day, when she came back inside, I'd wrap it from toe to elbow. She'd finally stopped trying to tease it down; being able to go out had made her more tolerant. Then, finally, three months after the accident, I decided to leave her unwrapped. By then, she was outside for a whole day anyway. Three months after the accident, she was back to her pre-disaster routine. She had an ugly scar on her upper arm, but most people wouldn't notice the slight swelling of her forearm. She seemed back to normal; but what would this mean for her future?

Spring arrived, and we suddenly had a two-year old! Once the ground had thawed and most of the mud subsided, I decided it was time to continue with her breaking. Breaking? My slow and painful method was more aptly called "boring." She'd been introduced to tack in the fall, before the accident, and had let me sit on her and walk up and down the barn aisle. Now, we'd take that outside.

Woody's round pen was a Godsend. I'd bring her in there, tacked up, and long-line her, running the two lines through the bit, through the stirrups, which I'd tied to the saddle, and back to me. She wasn't wild about it at first, but finally acquiesced; and we reached the point where she'd maintain a nice trot and do figure-eight's. Then, one day I drove her out the gate and around the big ring; and after a few days of this, I drove her out of the ring and off up the back road. This was my favorite part of training: I couldn't fall off if I was just walking behind her, and our dog could come along, too. She liked the change of scenery; and sometimes other boarders would ride along beside her. I set up my "training chart," too; just the way it was done at John Burke's barn. My plan was to duplicate John's training routines, so that when she actually went to the track, the transition would be smooth.

All during April, Millie and I did some kind of training. Most of the time, we started with long lines, and then, on April 17, I climbed on and rode her. Just in the round pen, and just for a few minutes, stopping, turning, backing up. On April 23, Millie's official second birthday, we measured her as a statuesque 15.1, and took more pictures, of course. In May, Doctor Orcutt came by and x-rayed her knees, declaring her ready for more advanced training. He was quite pleased by the look of her old scar, too; he thought she had a good pulse in that leg, and with time the scar would be less and less noticeable. Meanwhile, the training went on. On May 11, I started riding her in the big ring. It had a nice sandy track, a gentle oval that Woody used for his driving. Even though I was doing all this in painfully small increments, she was quite willful, and some days, downright ornery, so I started riding her with my friend Pam French and her pony, all this at a gentle trot, hoping this would encourage her. Some days, it did and she was an angel; other days, well … One day, she started feeling sticky, so I squeezed her with my legs, and she whipped her snaky neck around and bit my toe! Finally, May 20, I let her canter, and that seemed to improve her attitude. This was all short and sweet: the most we ever did was five circuits of the track, which I calculated to be just short of a mile. She never broke a sweat.

Millie in her own gate with Guy Henry.

Jim, meanwhile, was busy working on his contribution to the training of a future champion: a starting gate! He had four long 4x4 poles as corners, and rigged up a two-stall gate with hinges on the front doors, plywood sides and finally, the final touch, a sign across the front: Edgewood Downs! All painted a tasteful hunter green, it was a far cry from the giant metal monster that awaited her, but the general idea was there. After we'd done our laps, I'd ride her around the back of the old dairy barn, and we'd practice. We'd walk in with the front gates closed, we'd stand for a few minutes, and then Jim would yell, "Ring!" and open the fronts and we'd walk out.

Once school was out for the summer, my racehorse college began in earnest. I'd clip her to the back wall of the stall, tack her up, run polo bandages on all four legs, then bring her out, mount up, and do our laps. If Jim was around, we'd practice at the gate. I'd cool her out (just a little, since she never really heated up), wash her off, hose her legs the whole racetrack way. I thought this was fun; she was bored but cooperative. Then, on June 27, my blacksmith, Ricky Norris, stopped by the farm to put on the finishing touches: front shoes! I was almost crippled by anxiety, but she behaved fairly well.

July 6: This was it! All our careful planning, all our practicing, and today we loaded her into the trailer and headed for Rockingham Park, Barn D. John Burke was my trainer, of course; and I was still working for the summer as one of his grooms. She was one of my four charges. This year, John had acquired an in-house exercise rider, Guy Henry; and he assigned Guy to be her regular jockey. Guy was not only a wonderful person, but a patient, optimistic rider.

In my determination to give her the complete racetrack training, I'd forgotten one critical piece: mounting. Since I was at home working alone, I'd always mounted the old-fashioned way: foot in stirrup from the ground. At the track, though, the riders were given a leg up. The first day of her official training, I tied her to the wall, tacked her up, put polos on her legs, brought her out, and, holding her with my left hand, took Guy's ankle in my right and gave him a leg up. Bad idea! Out of the corner of her left eye, she saw a body rising up over her back, and exploded. It took ten minutes, and the help of John's assistant Joe Moore taking her back to the stall, to teach her the jockey method of mounting. I still owe Joe one watch, broken when she smashed Joe's arm into the stall screen.

RESOLVED: When preparing our horses for the track, make sure they learn about riders getting a leg up! Don't mount from the ground.

After that initial mounting fiasco, the rest of the summer was fairly quiet. She loved the nice soft footing on the track, loved being able to gallop along with other horses all around. I'd walk her to the track every day, and stand at the rail and watch her gallop. Guy was great; he was very patient with her, and after they came back, he'd give me a pole-by-pole account of how she went. She learned to stand for daily baths; eat out of a hay net in the front of the stall, get shod with racing plates, all the daily things that every racehorse, from her to Seattle Slew, went through.

At the end of August, Jim and I took a vacation to Saratoga, so I left her in the care of Curly, another of John's grooms. When I got back after our three-day break, Guy said she hadn't trained for two days. She had been pawing at the front of her stall, and banged her knee on her stall screen. The knee blew up, so John, being cautious, didn't train her. She got over that glitch, and I thought we were on course; but the next week, I noticed she seemed sore. Sure enough, her shins were bothering her. Her two-year-old year came to an abrupt end. I had to go back to school shortly, anyway; so we took her out of training and brought her home for the winter.

Millie training at Rockingham with Guy Henry and Leonard the pony.

The next spring, we started earlier. As soon as John and his crew came back from Florida and settled in at Suffolk, we sent her there. I was still teaching, so I'd race to the track and get her out before school, then fight the traffic to Cambridge and teach, and then head home to the farm. Suffolk was a much more urban setting than Rockingham: all the barns were lined up along the main road; there were no hidden nooks where you could graze a horse. Still, her routine was the same, and she settled right in. She tended to be wired all the time, of course; so I often took her between barns and let her mill around out there in the sun when I had the time. Finally, after she was fit enough, she had her first breeze, just three-eighths of a mile. She did fine, though, and when I got back to the barn, Donny Norton, one of the other grooms, said, "She did great! She could win for ten!" That's claiming, $10,000.

I smiled, but thought, "Ten?" Hah! We were convinced she was going to be a champion.

Looking back on her career, I find that some of my fondest memories are things that happened in the morning, far from the public eye. John had some very prominent owners at the time, and they had a filly they thought highly of. John orchestrated a work for her, a half mile, and decided she should work with Millie. That was fine with me; Millie could use the work, and working in company was always a good thing. The day of the work, the other horse set off with a jockey, and Millie with John himself in the saddle. I walked behind them to the track to watch, and the other filly's groom was with me. All the way to the apron of the grandstand, where we'd stand, she kept razzing me, "My filly's gonna blow Millie's doors off", that kind of thing. We stopped at a good vantage point. The two fillies galloped by us, then around the first turn and down the backside. When they got to the half mile pole, they started to breeze. Head to head, they raced into the turn, glued to the rail. It was a quiet morning out there; few other horses were near, and as they came out of the turn and headed down the stretch, we could hear their rhythmic breathing, and the soft sound of their hooves, and then, floating through the air as clear as crystal, John's voice: "I can't hold her! I gotta let her go!" and little Millie, ears pinned, pulled away from her companion. Yes, she "blew the doors off her." A sweet moment!

I remember that so vividly because sweet moments like that were few and far between. Millie had a long list of things she didn't like. Other people, for one: the starting gate, the people working in the starting gate, the blacksmith, the vet. She did like galloping in the morning, since the riders learned to let her alone; and she did like the quality of food at the track, and the deep bedding in her roomy stall. She did like working with another horse too, and gradually, the day arrived when she was ready to run. By then, it was summer, and we'd moved back to Rockingham. That was close to home, so I could be there in the morning, and then come back for feed time, too. Now that she was on the verge of making her debut, the question was, what race? John was a very successful trainer, a master at getting horses to run and knowing how to place them where they could win. He also knew me pretty well by then, too; so I got "the talk." He said that he'd run her in whatever race we wanted, but in his opinion, she should start in a claiming race where she'd compete with other fillies with similar ability; but, it was our call. Jim and I were adamant: claiming? No way! We'd seen her grow and mature, we'd seen her flying around in the field at home; we knew she was a winner! Her first race was not the race John had picked out, but one that we were sure would kick off her brilliant career.

The day arrived. I was late getting to the track; I'd had a sleepless night, and when I finally fell asleep, I overslept, and was vaguely nauseous, too. I took Millie out, cleaned her up, walked her around the shed, and then watched the clock, waiting for the time to bring her to the paddock. I was beyond-nervous. I'd had horses in my care run before, but this was the first time one of my own would be going to the paddock! A little before noon, I was sitting in the shedrow, and said to one of the other grooms, "Well, one thing for sure: she's never run before, but she is completely familiar with her jockey," since the jockey scheduled to ride her had been galloping and breezing her for weeks, and knew her thoroughly. No sooner had I said this than the loudspeaker went on: "John Burke! Call the Clerk of Scales. You need a rider for the fourth race." I think that my heart may actually have stopped for a beat. What???

Yes, on this Day of Days, Millie's trusty jockey had never shown up! John disappeared for a bit, and then came back to tell me her replacement:

Brent Kelly. Brent Kelly? I didn't know who that was, but Leslie, the pony girl, said I'd like him. With minutes to spare, off we went to the paddock.

Sin Mill heading to the paddock at Rockingham.
First foal / first race!

The paddock at Rockingham at that time was behind the grandstand, reached by walking up the track, past most of the grandstand, and then up a ramp which led through the building to the paddock in back. Millie had never been there; and I think the newness worked to our advantage. She was so curious that she was well behaved. She detested being saddled, of course: hated people on either side of her. John was quick and efficient, though, and we were soon going back through the tunnel onto the track.

I was so nervous for her (and our!) debut that I may have gone into a trance, but soon I heard, "They're off!" and her career was beginning.

Well, she was starting well: she burst quickly out of the gate and was right up with the leaders. Then, reality set in, and she was engulfed by the other horses. By the time they'd made the turn and were coming down the stretch, she trailed. John was right: she was outclassed.

When I was cooling her out, I felt so guilty for putting her in such a spot that I vowed to be realistic. No matter how they looked tearing around a field alone at home, they needed to be in races where they could be competitive. Millie was a proud filly; this was demoralizing for her, too. So, live and learn!

After she had two weeks to recover from that humiliation, she ran again, but this time at a lower level. She broke sharply, ran aggressively, and just missed. When we ran her back again, she won!

Seeing our little home-bred filly racing down the stretch in the lead and crossing the wire a winner was one of the highlights of our lives! If people could know that euphoric feeling, everyone in America would own a part of a horse: there is no feeling like it. Brent Kelly was our hero; he'd done a brilliant job humoring her throughout the race and bringing her home safe – and in front! She'd been so fractious in the gate that she'd managed to split one of his boots – but in the win picture, he was all smiles.

As I led her back from the winner's circle that day, bursting with joy, my friend, Mrs. Dudley, was standing on the rail, and yelled over to us, "Better enjoy it! These wins don't come that often!"

I turned to the friend walking with me and laughed. Hah! Obviously, she didn't know this winning filly. This was just the beginning.

Well, it was actually the beginning of the end. Millie was indeed competitive at that level, and she'd learned from these three races: she'd learned that she hated it. She hated the crowds, hated being saddled in the paddock, hated the starters leading her into the gate, hated the crush of a full field. If she could have made a living breezing against another horse in the morning, she would have been a success; but competing in a race in the afternoon just raised her hackles.

We were slow to admit defeat. She ran five more times, at Rockingham and Suffolk, but with each race, she became more difficult. One afternoon at

Suffolk we saddled her outside, thinking she'd be more accepting; and she bucked the whole saddle package over the hedge: saddle, pads, saddle cloth, girth – airborne! In the gate, she was getting dangerous. In the race, she just flew out of the gate, and as soon as she was in the clear, eased herself down. By then, her little brother Pete was beginning training, so we framed her one win picture and brought her home. John Burke would say, not quite facetiously, that one of his greatest feats as a trainer was getting Sin Mill to win a race!

Sin Mill: 8 starts / one win / one third

Rockingham Park Aug. 22, 1979 Six furlongs..1:15.3

9 SCHOOLHOUSE FARM J. J. BURKE, 3rd. **3-1**
BLACK & WHITE **SIN MILL** **113** BRENT KELLEY
Dark Green, Lime Belt and Bars on Sleeves
Ch.f.(1976). Millstone—Tenny Peche $3,250

2nd Evening Shoes   3rd Deweese

Petrifier (Pete)

When Sin Mill was a yearling, and Tenny was all rested up from her first foray into motherhood, we were so enamored of our little chestnut filly, so sure that she was destined for greatness, that we decided to try and duplicate her. That spring, we hitched up the trusty trailer and brought Tenny to a farm in West Newbury owned by Fred Craft. There, Millstone, sire of Sin Mill, held court.

Fred had given us the grand tour a few weeks before, taking Millstone out in the back field and letting him out on the end of the world's longest lunge line: 150 feet of parachute line. When Fred threw his hat in the air, the horse took off at a gallop, and for a few breathless minutes, tore around this huge circle at top speed, snatching mouthfuls of grass as he ran, bucking and kicking. It was an impressive display of athleticism; and the horse seemed to have a wonderful disposition, too. We were hooked. Now, we brought Tenny back for her second honeymoon with this handsome stallion. After she was settled in, Fred and Mary brought us into their kitchen for possibly the strongest cup of coffee I have had in my life. We sat in a little booth and talked, and finally I looked at Fred and asked about the stud fee. Jim, sitting next to me, saw Mary put her chin in her hand and raise three fingers beside her cheek. Fred looked at her, then me: "Well, how about three hundred?" Three hundred it was!

Now, a year later, Tenny was showing all the signs of imminent birth, so once again, I started my nightly checks. A lot had changed in two years: we now had a two-year old filly that we were convinced was a future champion, just waiting for the weather to stabilize to begin her serious training. She had survived the horrific ordeal of her mangled leg, and we were optimistic. The farm had changed, too: the cows were gone, and there were more boarders. It was no longer a quiet private farm, but there was still plenty of pasture space. We'd just survived the legendary Blizzard of 78 in our little house out back and all three of our horses were thriving.

The night of April 17, I brought Tenny in at feed time and noticed her udder was ominous, to say the least. We had dinner at the usual time, and I planned to check on her around 10:00 but after I'd done the dishes, I thought I'd just run over and see how she was doing, so Ringo and I walked down the back road in the dark. When I slipped in the back way, I saw she was already sweating and pawing. Within minutes, she lay down in the deep straw, and without further ado, began her serious labor. I slipped in beside her to help, but with only minimal encouragement on my part, a handsome foal rode a wave of water into the world. This time, Tenny was very aware of what was happening, and almost immediately got to her feet and spun around to look at the foal, nickering that wonderful mare-to-foal language that got him nodding his head and struggling to stand. Once again, I got that euphoric feeling of seeing a little creature appear into the world. A serene moment: this time, Tenny was very competent, hovering around and licking him. I toweled him off a little, and he started the bungling struggle to stand while Tenny positioned herself deliberately to help him find the waiting udder. A nice, normal foaling. When he seemed stable, I ran back to the house and summoned Jim, and he helped me iodine his navel. Yes, a colt! A full brother to Millie, but quite different: a dark bay, with no white socks; and a white patch on his forehead. Not quite a star; actually not unlike the fist-with-thumbs-down symbol. He had beautiful ears, shapely, and with the tips leaning toward each other, and a huge, liquid eye. Standing around in the stall, with the fragrant deep straw and the hovering mare, with the peace of the night outside: was there anything better? We were so glad we'd taken on this tilting at windmills.

The next morning, it was clear but chilly. We opened the door to the paddock, and Jim led Tenny out while I scooped up the foal and shuffled him out behind her. We left them out there for most of the day, and most of that time, Tenny picked at the early grass while he raced around. He seemed like a very active foal, and very healthy. Lots of the boarders came by, leaning on the fence and admiring him. My mother came by, too. She was not a horse person at all, so she drove by in her car and admired him from a discreet distance, then went to tell her friends in the bridge club that her daughter's horse had had a baby, and he was beige. Well, close.

Our second foaling seemed so much easier than the first. Maybe we were more relaxed, or just maybe this foal was going to make life easier for all of us. The next day, we repeated the turnout routine. Doctor Orcutt came by then, to check on the mare and her son; he pronounced the foal, "A beauty, nice short back!" When he was four days old, we turned them out in the big pasture; this time, with an added interest, another mare and foal. She was a big dark bay mare owned by Dr. Orcutt's assistant, Pat. Pat was an avid competitive trail rider, and Vigilette was the mare who had produced some of her best trail horses. This was a big help for everyone. With the two foals amusing each other, the two mares could relax and graze together. The two foals would play for most of the day, racing around much more than a foal by himself. They were so focused on each other, too, that they were less likely to hang around the fence line to interact with horses in the next pasture. My farm time was now taken up by working with Millie getting her ready to go to the track; I didn't hover around him the way I'd done with her. I was still teaching, too, and as soon as school closed for the summer, I went back to working at Rockingham. This foal was thriving on benign neglect.

Jim became our Namer of Horses. He had combined the Millstone and Tenny Peche names to come up with Sin Mill. Now, using the same combination, and the French angle of "peche", he produced "Petrifier," French for "turn to stone." We duly registered the foal with the Jockey Club as Petrifier, but to us, he was just plain Pete. There was no down side to this little guy: he learned to accept the halter and lead rope quickly; went to and from the pasture without a problem; got along with his pasture companion; was athletic, friendly, and photogenic. At six months, he was weaned. To me, the day of weaning was the hardest part of raising foals; I hated separating them from their mothers, listening to their pitiful cries, watching the mothers turn away as they were led off to another barn. It was heartbreaking. By the time he was ready for weaning, though, Pete seemed very independent, and almost indifferent to his mother. He'd only go to her for a quick drink; he'd spend his whole day with the other foal. This would be simple, right? Wrong! No matter how independent these foals seemed, when it came to be separated from their mothers, they were devastated.

Once again, my wonderful gelding Majorca saved the day. Pete was in the adjacent stall, and there was still a hole in the wall between them that Millie had enlarged. When Tenny disappeared and left Pete in his stall alone, Majorca immediately stuck his nose into the breach. Right away, Pete went to that corner, and that great warm muzzle jutting into his stall was an instant horse pacifier. Then, when it came time to go out to pasture, Majorca was once again the babysitter.

Once Pete was weaned, we were teetering on "horse poor." Millie was back from the track for the winter, so we were now using four stalls – paying board for four horses. We were so happy with our two homebreds, so sure that they would get to the races and win some serious money, that we weren't even close to worrying about it. On the contrary: we spent our winter months talking about what stallion to send Tenny to in the spring.

It amazes me to think, looking back, that we were bold enough to keep on with this plan. That spring, we sent Tenny to Maryland, to breed to a horse standing his first year at stud. He was unraced, but he was a son of the great Nijinsky. How could we pass that up? Now we had (1) my wonderful gelding, (2) a three year old filly (3) a yearling, and now (4) a mare in foal. Horse poor!

It was exciting, though: shipping her to Maryland on a big van. We took pictures, of course, of her walking on the van while our dog Ringo watched. We talked to the people at the Maryland farm; we got reports of the breeding and at last, confirmation that she was in foal. She arrived home to a hero's welcome.

Pete and Millie had made it through the winter without incident. Majorca and Pete went out together; Millie went out with Tenny until she left for Maryland. When the weather broke, I started getting Millie ready for her three-year old season at the track. Pete, in contrast to the eventful life Millie had led at his age, went through each day in a benign routine. When John Burke and his crew returned from Florida for the summer, Guy Henry visited us at the farm. He got on Millie for a gallop around the ring, rode her into our makeshift starting gate for us, and took a long look at Pete. He thought he was "absolutely gorgeous!" We thought so, too: much bigger than Millie, a beautiful mover, and well conformed.

Pete, at four months, was a handsome colt.

Pete's spring turned into summer, and then into fall: an endless series of days in the field with Majorca, and nights resting in his familiar stall. Once again, that fall we decided to enter the Yankee Thoroughbred Breeders yearling show. Millie did it, after all; we still had her third-place ribbon. Could Pete top that? One night we set up the trusty trailer at the barn and decided to teach Pete about that. Nothing attracts a crowd faster than a trailer lesson; and within minutes, all the boarders were standing around watching. I brought Pete out; he'd finished his supper after a long day in the pasture, and was relaxed. We walked up to the ramp; I stepped inside and showed him the full haynet that awaited. He'd follow me right in, right? Wrong! He froze, then tried to turn around, then backed up. One of the onlookers was standing nearby with a long dressage whip, so I asked to borrow that to encourage him. She handed it over, saying, "You break it, you buy it!"

Well, it only took two little taps with the whip, and Pete walked on. A little shaky, maybe; but he backed off quietly, and went on again. Lesson learned!

The show was on a Sunday morning. John Burke was still at Rockingham with all his horses, and once again let me use one of his empty stalls as a base, so we parked the trailer by his barn and settled Pete in to wait for the show. Pete was good; he loved the quality of the hay there, and was good about my brushing him off. John's crew was standing around admiring him and, jaded racetracker that I now was, I said to Jay Botty, "I hate doing this. There's always some idiot that lets his horse get loose."

After that snide remark, Pete and I headed off for the show. It was held right on the track in front of the grandstand. A small crowd was gathered to watch, including Jay and some others from John's barn. Pete was gawking at everything, but walked quietly beside me, following another yearling. The colt class was first, so we didn't wait long and the judge was decisive. Pete came in fourth!

We accepted the ribbon, and then walked back down the track toward the barn area. The other colts were all going that way, too and there was a line of fillies walking right at us, going to their class. When we got to the gap at the head of the stretch, Pete suddenly got agitated at all the fillies going in the opposite direction. He tried to spin around, and then reared. Really reared, straight up, with his front legs pawing the sky. One of his legs hooked the shank, and he backed up and fell over. I let go of the shank so that he wouldn't get tangled in it, but instead of getting right back up, he rolled over, away from me, and then leaped up and raced off. Fortunately, there were so many people around that he was quickly caught, and I sheepishly brought him back to John's barn. Of course, there was Jay, a big grin on his face: "So what idiot let his horse loose this time?" I'd never live that down!

As we headed into winter, I was back at school teaching, and the days were getting so short that my horse time was limited; I didn't have a lot of time to devote to his breaking. I did turn him out every day before school, so I started simply putting the tack on him, my exercise saddle and a simple snaffle, and leading him to the pasture tacked up. Then, I took the tack off at the gate, and he was off and running. It only took a minute or two, and this way, being tacked up was no cause for concern for him.

Pete was a quick study. When spring vacation came, I had a little more time, so I added to the routine. He quickly learned to work in the round pen, lounging at a walk, trot, and canter, and then, with the long-lines. He turned into a virtuoso at this: I could long-line him at all gaits, and then walk behind him and make him halt, back up, and then do side-passes. We had more boarders at the farm now, and they were impressed.

Pete in John Burke's barn at Rockingham.

When it came to carrying weight, he handled this with aplomb, too. I started getting on him in the round pen after his schooling session and riding him back to the barn, so he tolerated this well: my mounting meant he got to go in and eat. When I started getting on at the beginning of the sessions, he resisted at first. His protest took the form of rearing. He'd stand while I got on, pause, and then rear, really rear, straight up. That was it, then he'd settle down. It did get the attention of the boarders, though.

When summer came, school was out, so I could go back to Rockingham and work for John Burke again. Pete went with me. This time, his exercise rider would be Gary Ricci, and his career started off much more quietly than his older sister's. The others in John's shedrow liked him at once, liked his quiet ways, and his positive attitude on the track. After his flamboyant, emotional sister, he was easy to love.

Schoolhouse Farm was moving up: two horses in training at the track, and back home, a new foal.

We had a nice summer; I loved all the guys John had working for him, and loved my group of horses. Lots of camaraderie, and lots of wins for the barn. One morning, I drove to the track bright and early, as usual. I turned off the main road and drove behind the grandstand and I paused at the gap between the grandstand and the administration building to look through and see the horses training on the track, then continued to the barn. Just as I got out of the car, Gary Ricci came riding by and said, "There's a fire in the grandstand." Really? I'd just driven by there, so I pictured a little fire in a trashcan. I continued on to the barn and started getting Pete ready for his morning gallop. Suddenly, there was the sound of sirens, then the roar of fire trucks coming up the road. I walked outside, and when I looked toward the grandstand, it was ablaze! Everyone was stunned. Mercifully, the wind was carrying the smoke away from the backside, but it was a horrific sight. I brought Pete outside, and I still remember standing with him and looking toward the inferno. It was the end of Rockingham as we knew it.

Pete didn't make the races that year, but I wasn't expecting him to, really. After the Rockingham fire, John's whole team moved to Suffolk, and he went with them to John's barn there. It was one of the new barns, and he settled right in. A bonus: they parked one of the starting gates right outside the barn, so I'd take Pete over and lead him through and make him stand. I did not want another horse who acted up in the gate. After he trained, and had cooled out, I'd bring him over there and just mess around for a while, trying to get him to be relaxed about this huge iron cage.

Pete was well behaved, but he was a worry-wart. I was using Mark Perry as an exercise rider; he referred to him as "the rail," because he was, for his size, narrow. Mark was terrific: always gave me lots of feedback, and was very professional. He was also very busy. From the time the track opened until it closed for training, he almost never touched the ground, jumping off one horse and onto another. I had my pre-arranged time; if he came in and Pete wasn't tacked and waiting, he kept going. Thanks to him, I am to this day very quick at tacking up. After training, Mark would go to Waldeck's, the tack shop, and I'd always see his gear over there: chaps neatly folded, and his boots clean and shining. To this day, when I clean my boots after a ride, I think of Mark.

When his training intensified, Pete became anxious. He was slow to eat, picked at his hay and then really backed off on feed. This was not good, so John suggested we take him off the track for a while. Once again, we relied on our old friends, the Roches. They had that nice training track, and we thought he could keep going, but relax, so off he went. That worked. Country air worked its miracles, and after a few weeks, he was ready to return.

When he was close to running, John had "the talk" with me once again. Now that school was in session, I wasn't working for him. Pete was still in his barn, but he was the only horse I had time for. John said it was time for me to get my trainer's license. I was shocked. I had never really considered it, but John said I'd put in the years, and was pretty much training Pete myself anyway, so he was confident that I was ready.

Being a teacher myself, I was constantly giving tests, but it had been years since I'd had to take one. When I went to the Horsemen's Association office for the written part, I was a nervous wreck. I passed that, then the barn test was an automatic "pass," since John was the one who gave that test. Finally, I had to take the stewards' test, which was much longer and more detailed. Again, I was a bundle of nerves but I managed to pass that, too.

When Pete appeared in the program, I'd be listed as his trainer, and our "Schoolhouse Farm" listed for breeder and owner.

Finally, the day of Pete's debut arrived. Although I'd sworn, after Millie's debut, to be realistic about our horses, we let him run at the top maiden level. Well, he was well behaved in the paddock, although I could tell he was nervous, but he was outrun. We ran him again, with the same results. The third time he ran, we needed a jockey at the last minute. The one we ended up with was someone I didn't know, but he came well recommended. Pete was good in the paddock, again, and then went onto the track with his pony girl, Cathy Chumbly. I watched anxiously from the apron as the horses all warmed up and then went back to the starting gate. I didn't have binoculars, so it was hard to see the horses loading, but just as I thought they were ready, we heard an announcement: "Number seven, Petrifier, has been scratched." What?? I had no idea what had happened. I knew he'd warmed up, and I saw Cathy leading him behind the gate but what could have gone wrong? The race went off without him. I could see him behind the gate, without the jockey, being held by Cathy, and as soon as the race was over, she brought him back, jogging happily, and soundly, beside her pony. She was mad. She said everything was fine, but as they turned to go to the gate, he tripped, and the jockey started yelling for the vet, swearing he was breaking down, so the vet scratched him.

I was relieved that he was fine, but realized that he was now on the vets' list, and he hadn't even won a race. As I led him off the track, I met one of the practicing vets and asked him to take a quick look. He agreed, too, that he was fine. A few days later, I made an appointment with the track vet, Dr. Decker, to have him work in front of him. Leslie, John's pony girl, suggested I use a jockey, and she mentioned Tony Barreira. I didn't know Tony, but he was available, so that morning I tacked Pete, gave Tony a leg up, and we walked to the track. Dr. Decker was standing on the rail, so I joined him, pointing out Pete as he and Tony galloped their way to the backside. Right on cue, they slipped into a breeze, and swept by us, looking terrific. When they pulled up and jogged off the track, Dr. Decker asked how he'd felt, and Tony, the honest person he was, said, "Oh, he feels great; but the horse I'm riding in the fourth race today?"

Pete was off the vets' list and I'd found my new jockey. I entered him again, only this time at a more realistic level. When I saw the other entries in the race, my heart sank. The great Alan Jerkens was sending up a horse from New York! Naturally, he was the heavy favorite. Oh well, maybe Pete could come in second. Two days later, we prepared for battle. I enlisted my good friend, PeeWee, one of John's grooms, to take him to the paddock. We marched up there together and met Tony, who was cheerful and optimistic. Pete was fairly relaxed, too. The crowd was betting heavily on Alan Jerkens' horse, so there was little expectation for us.

When the gates opened, it seemed like everything went in slow motion. I watched from the apron as the field ran down the backside and could see Pete inching his way to the lead. They turned for home, and he still looked good and when they straightened out for the run to the wire, he pulled away. We were euphoric! Once again, we experienced that feeling-like-no-other to see our homebred coming down the stretch in front of a wall of horses. For us, our second foal, and our second winner, we felt as if we'd already beaten the odds.

After the race, when I'd gradually returned to earth and returned Pete from the test barn to his stall in John's stable, Peewee greeted me with a huge smile. "Well done, Mrs. Alan Jerkens!" he laughed. From that day on, he'd call me that. An added bonus of that race was its payoff: since Alan Jerkens' horse was so heavily favored, and since Pete was, to put it kindly, undistinguished, and trained by an unknown, the winning payoff was huge. Jim was never a big bettor, but he made enough in that race to treat anyone in the area to dinner.

Pete, July 1980 at "The Rock," with Gary Ricci.
Days later a fire destroyed the grandstand and closed the track.

Pete's career was not really distinguished, but it was long. He ran his last race as an eight-year-old, and spent most of that time at the racetrack. When we had decided it would be "fun" to raise a racehorse, and then another, and another, we hadn't thought about the exponential increase in expenses. When Pete won his first race, we had three others at home: Millie, his mother, and his new brother. "Home" to us was the farm we lived on, but it wasn't our farm, so every horse we had there had to pay board. Every cent of Pete's earnings had to pay not only his feed and vet bills, but the board for his family. He did what most racehorses do: eked out a living. He didn't make lots of money, but when he ran, what he made helped defray all the expenses at home. At that time, Suffolk Downs raced year round so he stayed at the track through the winter. It was actually easier to deal with him there, for one; and winter racing still generated a little income. He was quite cheerful living on the backside and was never a problem.

No, his career was not distinguished, but he stayed amazingly sound. He did toe out a little, and he went through a period where he'd hit his ankle. Solving that problem involved some creative bandaging and fiddling with shoeing, until we eventually got over that bump in the road. He wasn't an aggressive horse; he only really ran well when he was on the outside, and the track surface was to his liking. Tony continued to ride him for a long time, until he relocated. Then Jack Penney took over, and when he left for other tracks, Pete's current exercise rider, Henry Ma, also a jockey, took over the job as his "pilot." It was Henry who rode him for his last win, at the age of eight.

Petrifier: 47 starts / 7 wins/ 1 second/ 4 thirds

Tony Barreira brings Pete home to the Winner's Circle.

```
         "3-M Quick Printers Purse"
                PETRIFIER
   Owner          Suffolk Downs        6.Furlongs
   School House Farm                   A.Barriera
   Trainer        2nd.Sid's Ambition   Time 1:16.3
   Susan Walsh    3rd.Speedy Brave     March 14,1982
```

```
                    Petrifier
Owner               Suffolk Downs          6.Furlongs
School House Farm                          A.Barreira
Trainer             2nd.Mystic Joe         Time 1:15.1
Susan Walsh         3rd.Let 'Em Hum        Nov.15,1982
```

```
                    PETRIFIER
Owner              Suffolk Downs           1 Mile
School House Farm                          Jack Penney
Trainer            2nd.Mysterious Chuck    Time 1:43.1
Susan Walsh        3rd.Dark Streak         March 13,1983
```

```
              PETRIFIER
Owner             Suffolk Downs      6.Furlongs
School House Farm                    Jack Penney
Trainer           2nd.My Copy        Time 1:16.2
Susan Walsh       3rd.Topnotching    Dec.30,1983
```

```
                    PETRIFIER
Owner               Suffolk Downs       6.Furlongs
School House Farm                       Henry Ma
Trainer             2nd.Who's Ugly      Time 1:14.1
Susan Walsh         3rd.Cut The Chatter May 5,1986
```

He's Dansin (Dansin)

Early spring at the farm. Tenny was now expecting her third foal, and we were wildly excited. Her first foal, Millie, had won a race at Rockingham, which was the most emotional experience of our lives to date, and her second foal, Pete, was showing promise in his training at Suffolk Downs. Still, one win had not begun to tip the financial scale over to the black; and we now had four stalls at the farm. There was Tenny, though, growing bigger by the day. I came home from school and took her for walks up the back hill for exercise, and we were thrilled to see a full-page ad in the *Bloodhorse* for the stallion, Masked Dancer, son of the great Nijinsky, grandson of the legendary Northern Dancer. Jim was already dreaming up combinations of names for the new foal.

It was late in April. Millie and Pete were both April foals, which seems to work well in New England, but this foal was now almost a month overdue. We'd moved Tenny from the big barn to the stallion barn to await the birth, and with the ominous signs of her udder, I'd begun nightly checks.

April 26: I checked on Tenny after dinner, then planned to run down again around 10:00. I went to bed early, lulled by the sound of the wind and rain on our rustic house. Suddenly, I woke up, and realized it was much later than I'd planned, almost midnight. I threw on a coat and shoes, and Ringo and I made the trip down to the barn. When I opened the door, I knew I was too late: there was no mistaking that salty, steamy aroma of labor and birth. I walked quietly down the aisle and peered into her stall. She was lying flat-out in the straw, her belly looking huge. I thought, Maybe she's still in labor. Maybe, but just then, from behind the bulk of her body, up popped a set of tiny, curious ears. Then, a whole head, a shock of black forelock, wide liquid eyes, a prominent white blaze. Tenny heard us, and leapt to her feet. The afterbirth fell to the straw with a rush, and the foal jumped to his feet too.

The foal was stunning. He'd already figured out how to nurse, which he did readily, and Tenny was obviously enamored of her new son.

Euphoric, I ran back to the house and woke Jim, saying: "She's had her foal. It's a colt – and he looks just like Northern Dancer!" We returned to the barn and gazed on the two of them, basking in the sight, relieved that he'd finally arrived, convinced that he was, indeed, the reincarnation of his great grandfather, Northern Dancer. He was bigger than Millie and Pete, and had a real presence.

The next day, we got them out in the paddock, but the weather wasn't cooperating. It was gloomy and misty, with drizzle from time to time, so we hovered around and brought them back in when it got worse. When they were out, a solid stream of boarders walked by to admire the newest addition to the farm, and one of them, Gerry Fitz-Gerald, presented Tenny with a beautiful horseshoe-shaped wreath of dried flowers for her stall door. Moving them in and out was infinitely easier than it was with Tenny's first foal, since now she knew the routine. The weather was dicey for the next few days, but it finally warmed up and got more predictably sunny. For the most part, things went smoothly. We had a little snag to begin with: the foal seemed to breathe faster than he should, so we took his temperature and found it slightly elevated, and called Dr. Orcutt to check him out. This time, though, it was not "Doc" but his son. Doc was the classic horse doctor, his son definitely an equine practitioner. He was very analytical, but he had the same instincts of his father. He was not particularly worried about the foal; he did bloodwork, and after a few days of worry on our part and nonchalance on the foal's, things seemed to normalize.

When we switched them to the big pasture, they entered a blissful stage of their lives. There was another mare, a handsome Standardbred, to keep Tenny company, and her foal was a buddy for ours. They stayed out most of the day, and the weather was idyllic. Jim came up with a name. Combining the sire and dam, Masked Dancer and Tenny Peche, he declared him "He's Dansin." So, Dansin it is!

Dansin seemed to grow bigger by the day. Watching him race around with his buddy, we marveled at the fluidity of his stride. He was a cheerful boy, too, and when we started feeding him solid food in the stall, Tenny was kind to him. With Pete and Millie, she was pushy, so we'd had to tie her up just to let the foal feed. Not this guy! He'd go right to his little foal feeder, and she'd stay at her tub in the other corner.

One day in August I drove up late in the day, just in time to see the two mares and the foals down at the bottom of the pasture. The mares stood waiting to come in, while the two foals raced around. As I watched, Dansin tore around right behind the other mare, and like lightning, she bucked and kicked out with both hind legs. Her hocks scooped him up as he ran by, and lifted him in a big arc, sending him sailing through the air to land in a heap. As I stood in shock, he paused for a split second, then leapt up, shook himself, and raced off, unharmed.

Except for that brief heart-stopping moment, his first six months of life unrolled without incident. We often paused when they were in for the night to watch him in the stall. One night, Jim ominously noted that, while he was eating, he'd take a mouthful of food, then circle around Tenny and go back for another bite.

"You don't think he's a stall walker, do you?" I shrugged it off. John Burke had had a horse who was brilliantly fast, but a determined stall-walker; and that vice drove John and everyone else in the barn to the brink. I wouldn't wish that on anyone.

Six months slipped by as smoothly as any breeder could want. When weaning time came, we moved the two back to the stud barn, and the next day, when I brought them in for the night, I made a U-turn with Tenny and took her back to the big barn, leaving Dansin alone. I always hated this part of horse rearing and Dansin was just as heartbroken as the others. There was no Majorca next door to provide comfort, either. He paced restlessly, whinnying piteously; finally, we shut off the lights and hoped he'd settle down overnight.

The next morning, he was still restless. When I got to the barn and looked in at his stall, I was stunned: there was a definite track through the shavings, and there he was, going around and around. Now that he had the stall to himself, he had the room to do what Jim had suspected: stall-walk.

He was inconsolable. I fed him his breakfast, but he just kept circling. The hay I'd put in was strewn everywhere, but the scariest part was the look in his eye: a blank, deranged stare. So, what to do? We'd thought of keeping him in his stall until he seemed over his weaning, but by the way he was going, he'd wear himself out. I opened the door to the paddock and led him out. He actually staggered, took a few dizzy steps, then stopped, and promptly fell asleep.

A stall walker. I thought back to all that John Burke had gone through with the horse he'd had, and felt almost overwhelmed. Where did this come from? Millie and Pete showed no tendency to do this, nor Tenny. If he was in fact a stall walker, we'd just try to eliminate the stall.

Now that he was weaned, we moved him back to the big barn, right next to Majorca. Majorca was my secret weapon: he had raised Pete and Millie after they'd been weaned, and now he took right over. The little hole in the wall between their stalls had gradually grown larger, and now, at night, Dansin parked himself right there, with Majorca a breath away on the other side and this new phase of his life began. Out all day, as early as possible to as late as possible, with his friend Majorca; then in for the night with his nose stuck into Majorca's stall. Being out all day, he was tired and relaxed when he came back in, so, hopefully, he'd just rest quietly at night.

After a few months, the hole in the wall became so big that Dansin could put his whole head through. One day, my blacksmith, Rick Norris, stopped in, and I was giving him the tour of the barn. The first stall on the left was Majorca's, so we looked in there. Majorca was standing against the back wall, and Dansin's little head was stuck through the hole. Dansin was actually asleep, his eyes closed. Ricky peered in and cried, "What the hell is that?" He thought for a second that it was some kind of stuffed horse-head.

This routine seemed to work. Being out all day, Dansin was tired by the time he came in, and with that ever-growing hole in the wall, he was never really by himself. They went out no matter what the weather. One day, a photographer from the local paper came by during a storm and took a picture of Majorca and Dansin racing through the snow. That picture made the front page.

That winter, as Dansin was heading toward his yearling year, was a cold one; but Dansin had a thick mane and grew a lovely heavy fur coat, so bad weather was not a problem for him. At that time, there was a series of pipes that carried water into each stall, and Woody had his crew cover the fronts of the stalls with plastic to keep in the warmth. One morning, I was the first to get to the barn. I walked up to the big front doors, slid them open, and stopped: what was that noise? It sounded like someone taking a shower.

I was right. I walked down the aisle, following the noise right to Dansin's stall, opened his door and was greeted by a horrific sight: the pipe carrying water to his bucket had burst, and cold, icy water was spewing forth. Dansin was cowering in the far corner, but he was soaking wet, and the spray was sluicing down his heavy coat.

I somehow managed to shut off the water quickly, and ran to get blankets. Dansin was so cold that he stood shuddering while I scraped him off and covered him as best I could, toweling off his head and wrapping his neck, too. The stall was soaking wet, of course; inches of cold water everywhere. Kenny Brown, Woody's right-hand man, walked in just as I'd covered Dansin from ears to tail, and immediately took over. I held Dansin in the aisle out of the way while he stripped the stall, throwing the sodden bedding down the manure hole and re-bedded it with dry shavings. Then, Dansin went back in. I changed his blankets and tried to towel him off as vigorously as I could, to try and restore some circulation to his frozen body. It was an absolutely frigid day, so turning him out was not an option and he was so cold that stall-walking for once wasn't either.

Amazingly enough, he survived. After a while, he loosened up and ate the hay I offered and settled at the back of the stall where he could peer in at Majorca. The sun coming through his window helped, too and the stall seemed to warm up. The next day? He was fine; he went out with Majorca and simply went on with his life.

The farm was changing rapidly. When we'd had our first foal, they had just sold off the cows, but the Welsh pony herd was huge. Now, there were only a few ponies left, and little by little, it was becoming a boarding stable. We were using five stalls now, so we had some clout but it was more difficult to do things when and where we wanted. That spring I was visiting my old friend John Roche and mentioned that it was time to start breaking Dansin, and now that there were more boarders, it was going to be tricky. John's daughter Cathy had a boyfriend who was there that day, John Rodger. He was a jockey with worlds of experience, but he genuinely loved breaking babies. He heard us talking, and immediately volunteered.

The next day, the farm was its usual beehive of activity. There were boarders riding in the ring, and others tacking their horses up, standing around criticizing the ones riding: the usual weekend at the farm. Then, up drove John. He came roaring up to the barn in his ancient, huge boat of a Cadillac and strode over to us. He had an old tweed cap on his head, ancient paddock boots, and jeans. All the boarders in their riding attire immediately pricked their ears. We went into the barn, where I had just brought Dansin in. I had already been putting tack on him, and he was relaxed about that; so we went into his stall and John had me give him a leg up, to lie across his back. He did that a few times, and then we went out to the round pen. All the boarders gathered in clumps by the side of the big ring. In the round pen, John took off his cap, turned it around, slammed it back on, and I gave him a leg up. He did that for a few minutes, lying across the saddle, me leading Dansin around. Then, quickly, without further ado, John swung all the way up into the saddle. Dansin raised his head, cocked his eye back, and then just kept circling. We made a few circuits of the ring, and John said, "Turn me loose." I did, and the two of them picked up a trot. They made a few circuits of the ring, turned, made a few the other direction and then John said, "Open the gate!"

I opened the gate, and John simply rode out into the big ring and then the two of them went sailing off. The big ring had a sand track Woody used for driving, and John and Dansin went jogging off around that as if they'd done it a million times. Clumps of boarders stood by in silence: no more comments about his odd car, his unorthodox "position", his lack of helmet.

After a few minutes, John pulled up at the gate, hopped off, and simply said, "Smart horse. Be back tomorrow."

That was that. John came over every day for a week or so, taking Dansin around the big ring at a jog, and then a slow canter. I was amazed: did someone already break him without our knowing? Was he a racehorse in a previous life? He took to it eagerly.

John Rodger teaching Dansin to gallop at Roche's Farm.

When school was out in June, I had the time to bring Dansin to the track. We brought him first over to Roche's farm. John Rodger was over there every day, and they had a good training track, with deep sand, where he could really learn to gallop. John was an absolute wizard with young horses. Dansin, just a green two-year-old, was galloping at their track with his neck bowed, looking as aggressive and eager as an experienced race horse. He stayed there for two weeks, getting fit, learning the routine and then it was time to go to the track.

My old Kingston trailer was still road-worthy. Jim had sanded it all down and painted it in our racing colors: a tasteful dark green with a light green stripe. In spite of his stall walking, Dansin didn't seem to mind the confinement of a trailer. He had walked right on at first asking (as soon as he'd spotted the haynet waiting for him inside), and rode quietly. Maybe the motion of the trailer satisfied his desire to keep moving. At any rate, he had been fine on the short trip from our farm to Roche's, and now, he handled the long ride from there to Suffolk Downs – with all its stops, heavy traffic and road noise as if, again, he'd done it all in a previous life. He was now officially registered with the Jockey Club as "He's Dansin," and in residence at Suffolk Downs. Three foals, and now three horses-in-training!

He's Dansin with jockey Jorge Vargas coming back from his first win.

Dansin's racing career could be a book of its own. As we had discovered when he was just a foal, he was a stall-walker, possibly the world's greatest stall-walker. As long as he was at the farm, we could manage it: he'd go out at first light and stay out until sundown. When he finally went back to his stall, there was a huge hole between his stall and his buddy's, and he could stick his whole head and neck in there for comfort. At the track, though, it was a different story. Suffolk Downs was an urban track: no little paddocks, no grazing areas, just lines of barns. Every horse there had his own stall, and every stall had a roof. Dansin seemed to enjoy being there: galloping on the track, cooling out after training, munching on his hay, watching others in the barn, getting a bath outside, but periodically, like clockwork, he'd be standing in his stall and his eyes would glaze over, he'd turn around, and then circle, faster and faster, until he was exhausted. The training was no problem: John Rodger had done a great job galloping him on the farm, and he enjoyed the wide-open spaces of a full-sized race track. Mark Perry was his exercise rider, and he looked forward to his daily gallops. We were encouraged by the progress he was making in training; it was the idle hours in his stall that were the problem. His shoes, standard aluminum training plates, were taking a beating. I still have a shoe from one of those days. The right side looks unused, but the left side was so worn down by his circling that it looks like lacy tinfoil. He was losing weight, too in spite of eating everything in sight.

A few years earlier, John Burke had had a bad stall-walker. That horse had tons of talent, blinding speed, but he'd been worn down by his activities inside the stall. I remembered what John went through with him, so I didn't bother trying some of the "cures" that hadn't worked with that horse. I was never out of suggestions, though; everyone who walked through the barn had something to offer, and I tried them all. The first few were relatively easy. Hang a board in the stall, so he couldn't circle without interruption. That worked for a day, and then he figured out how to bump the board just enough to swing it out of the way. It was dizzying just watching. Then, fill the stall with tires, blocking his path. That worked momentarily and then he figured out how to work through the tires like some Navy Seal in training. Hang three tires from the rafters, where he couldn't make a circle without running into them. Fine, but he managed to bump them and get them swinging, and then timed his circles to fly through the arc. Then, of course, there was the morning when I got there to find him standing at the door with his head through one of the tires, the tire hanging around his neck like some rubber horse collar. Next, a mirror: trick him into thinking there was a horse there he could see. I got an unbreakable mirror so clear that it did look like a hole in the wall. He ran over, saw himself, and started heavy breathing. Within seconds, it was all steamed up and with the image obscured, he went back to his circling.

The fitter he got, the faster he went. After a few weeks, he could canter, flying around and around until he exhausted himself. One day, the trainer on the backside offered a suggestion: hobbles. "Old Cajun trick," he said, and threw an old set of reins over his back. He made a loop out of another set of reins, and joined the two together. The loop circled Dansin's upper legs, above the knee, and constricted his stride. Hah! Problem solved! I had a wonderful afternoon hanging around the barn, watching Dansin standing at the front of his stall, eating hay like a normal horse. Finally, I left for the day.

The next morning, I came into the barn before dawn. It was now fall, and I was back teaching, so I got to the track very early, to get Dansin out before I had to go to school. The barn was quiet. I didn't hear the usual patter of feet as he tore around his stall, but there was some kind of thumping: he had somehow figured out how to run around in circles with his front legs held together. He looked like some bizarre bay kangaroo.

Dansin was a creative horse, for sure, and also unusually limber. I tried tying him at the front of the stall, but when the mood came over him, he manage to circle, even tied up, by just wringing his neck. Then, I tied him on both sides. After a day or so, he could still back up and circle, and screw his head around, as the two ropes twined together. I could tell how many times he'd circled by counting the number of times the two ropes were twisted.

I was under time constraints now, too; I had two horses at the track, Dansin and his older brother Pete, so I had to have help getting them out before school. Mark Perry's wife Eileen was willing to lend a hand. She had a job working with Dr. Sheehan, but she didn't start that job until I'd gone to school, so she could be there at the crack of dawn to help out. This worked well, since Mark got both my horses out early. Eileen was watching all my failed attempts at "curing" the stall-walking and came up with another solution.

I came into the barn one morning, and there she was, standing beside Dansin's stall with a friend, a large, friendly goat named Jerry. She'd taken him on trial from another trainer and reasoned that Dansin would rather stand around with his goat than stall-walk. This could work! Dansin was already hovering all over him and the goat seemed to like the attention. After he'd trained and cooled out, we put him back in his stall with his new friend. Eureka! The two just milled around, munching hay, breathing on each other, watching the activities in the shedrow. It was the answer to my prayers.

The next day, I walked into the barn in the early morning silence. Silence, except for the patter of feet. Sure enough, Dansin was tearing around his stall as usual, and now he had a companion, a galloping goat.

That cure only worked for a day, but long enough for Dansin to get very attached to his shaggy friend; so I had to buy the goat. He stayed at the front of the stall, out of the way of Dansin's feet, but within reach. Dansin didn't mind leaving him while he went to the track, but he'd better be there when he got back.

Somehow, during all this angst about his stall walking, Dansin kept training. Finally, he was fit enough to breeze, so we decided to have Mark let him breeze an easy 3/8. By his schedule, this had to be early, so one morning Eileen and I followed Mark as he rode him to the track. We stood at the gap, and they set off in the dark. It was so early that few horses were out there, so early that we could only see horses as they flashed by in the dark. We waited, watched a few others pass, and then, through the gloom, we saw his distinctive blaze coming at us. In seconds, he appeared, flew by, and disappeared down the stretch. Well, what we saw looked good, but we waited anxiously for Mark to come back. When he rode off the track toward us, he was beaming: "He can fly!"

Once he got that first breeze over, things picked up fast. He did gate work, and oddly enough, he was completely relaxed in that big metal cage, and got his gate card easily. His works continued, and most were good. Most were from a running start, and the times were nice. From the gate, it seemed to take him longer to get in gear, but we were pleased. Now, we'd always thought he was meant for the turf. He was a grandson of the great Nijinsky, and I'd found a picture of Nijinsky himself as a two-year old: they could be twins. He had the classic turf feet, too: round, flat and enormous. I have a picture of him taken in the paddock that looks like his legs are stuck into upside-down plant pots. His first race would be on the dirt, though; there weren't any maiden turf races scheduled.

Dansin's goat Jerry with our dog Rooney.

This was the year that our fledgling Mass Thoroughbred Breeders Association was going to have stakes races, too. One of them was for three year old and most of the horses eligible had had little experience, so we entered him. I felt we should support our program, for one, and the purse was to us enormous. It would also probably be a small field, and a good place to start, even though it was on the dirt, so we couldn't test our "made for the turf" theory.

For a horse who was so terrifying to watch when he was in one of his stall-walking frenzies, he was in all other respects very relaxed. His first trip to the paddock was uneventful; he was curious, but stood quietly surveying the crowd while he was being saddled. Vernon Bush was the jockey we'd named. He had worked him for us, and seemed to get along with him. He was also a superior rider, with excellent instincts and lots of experience.

Dansin was relaxed, but Jim and I were nervous wrecks. Jim decided to stay out of the paddock, and was standing by the fence, camera at the ready, when the jockeys came out. Dansin was standing quietly, Vernon came over to us and I noticed immediately something odd.

"Vernon, what have you got on?" I asked, looking at the silks, which were blue and green squares with a big yellow dump truck on the front.

Vernon looked down. "What? Isn't this you – Schoolbus Farm?" Not quite!

My old mentor, John Burke, was standing at the fence, and noticed the silks right away. He also saw Jim focusing his camera and said to his comrades, "Watch the guy with the camera when he sees the jockey." Sure enough, Vernon was getting in range, Jim was focusing on him to capture this moment for posterity, and suddenly lowered the camera with a stunned look on his face. "What the…"

Well, Dansin was none the wiser and what silks he wore wouldn't matter to the outcome of the race, so I gave Vernon a leg up, and he joined the others in the post parade. Everything from then on went fine: Dansin warmed up well, walking right into the gate, and they were off. He ran well: he was in mid-pack for a while, then down the stretch smoothed out and gained ground, and ended up finishing fourth, behind the three horses everyone had picked. We had no complaints; he came back cheerfully, went back to the barn for his bath, and dove into his dinner.

The day after his debut, Dansin was his old self. The race had taken nothing out of him. A week later, they scheduled another maiden race, and this time it was on the turf. We decided to seize the moment and entered him. We couldn't have Vernon ride him, though; he'd been injured that week, and had to sit it out, so we named Jorge Vargas, another solid, competent rider. He'd never ridden Dansin in the morning, but for such a professional, experienced rider, that didn't matter.

The day of the race, the weather turned cloudy, and showers were forecast. I was a nervous wreck: Suffolk had to baby their turf course in order to make it through the whole season in good shape, so if there was rain, they'd often take the races off the turf. All morning, I fretted, listening to every forecast, but the race stayed on the turf.

Once again, we made the trip from the barn to the paddock, walking in a line of horses entered for that race. I walked up with Dansin, and my friend PeeWee led him up. Peewee was as calm as I was nervous; he'd run so many horses over the years that he realized that being nervous was pointless. Dansin's odds were long. There were a few favorites in the race, and he'd never been on the turf course, so even though we "knew" he was meant for the turf, it had yet to be proven. Once again, he was good in the paddock, warmed up well, walked into the gate and they were off! The turf course was inside the dirt course, so its circumference was smaller. To make the distance to the wire, the gate was positioned at the head of the stretch, so I watched as the field broke from the gate and came thundering by, with that thrilling sound of horse's hooves on turf. Dansin was at the rear of the group, but as they went by for the first time, Jim grabbed my arm: "He loves it! He loves the turf!"

It was true: he was moving much differently than when he breezed on the main track, gliding along with his hind legs, throwing his front legs in front, with those enormous hooves flinging out ahead of him. They passed us in a blur, made the first turn, ran down the backside, and he was still well in the rear but as they came out of the final turn, we could see him looming on the outside, and little by little, gaining on the leaders. When they reached the wire, I just wanted to hold that moment, to freeze it forever: our bizarre stall-walker, our homebred, home-raised third foal of our only mare – sailing home in front!

Jubilation was an understatement! Most of the people at the track had known how quirky this horse was, how much we'd gone through trying to figure out his compulsion to stall-walk, so we were surrounded by well-wishers. Dansin was unruffled by all the excitement. He behaved well in the test barn, stood for a bath, and when he was cooled out, was reunited with his constant companion, Jerry the goat. I was stunned: our mare had had three foals to run, and now they were all winners, quite an accomplishment! We had been raising horses now for eight years, and most of the time it was a constant battle to pay bills. The purse money from this race would help, but more than that, it gave us the hope that Dansin would actually win enough races to get us ahead.

We knew now that our hunch about his ability on the turf was proven correct, so we were determined to keep him on grass. Two weeks later, there was a race suited to him: a race for horses who had only won one race, an allowance race, on the turf. It was scheduled for the same day as the Massachusetts Handicap, Suffolk's premier race. That day was the peak of the meet: horses would be shipping in from other tracks for the MassCap, and there would be a huge crowd. That didn't bother us; Dansin didn't mind excitement, and the timing was right so, he was entered. We had Jorge Vargas again, since he'd ridden him to victory, but it was a tough field of serious horses. Once again, I spent the morning pacing around, watching the ominous clouds but the race stayed on the turf, so off we went.

This race was almost a replay of the other turf race: he broke with the field, but strode away from the gate in a leisurely fashion, so he was last most of the way. Then, coming around the far turn, he started accelerating, gaining on the leaders with every stride. At the wire, he was a fast-closing third. We were thrilled. We both ran down to the track and cheered him as he pulled up. Jorge caught my eye, unsmiling, and said, "He stumbled bad on the backside." That didn't stop my grinning and cheering, so he said it again, "He stumbled bad!"

Peewee and I took him back to the barn, gave him a bath, and took turns walking him out. I was still excited by how well he did but after a few minutes of walking, the excitement faded fast. He was sore. His stride shortened, and after a while, he was favoring his left. We stopped to look closer, and sure enough, there was a knot on his tendon, a swelling which seemed to grow as we watched. We took him outside the barn, and Peewee grabbed a cold hose while I ran for the vet. Marty Simensen, our brilliant veterinarian, was quick to arrive, and quick with a diagnosis: when Jorge said he'd stumbled, he'd rapped his tendon. The cure? Bute for now, to contain the swelling, but some serious time off. While our little drama was playing out, the races were still going on and, as we stood there watching the swelling grow, there was a deafening roar from the grandstand. Peewee and I exchanged glances: we knew right away what that meant. Bill Perry, a local trainer, had just won the MassCap with his horse Let Burn! This was the reality of racing: the thrill of a victory and the agony of, in this case, a tendon.

So ended Dansin's three year old debut. We brought him home immediately, to turn him out and let the leg heal. I dreaded the thought of his stall walking with that injury, so we came up with a plan. The barn at the farm was a huge, three-story bank barn. The main floor was all stalls, but the cellar was empty and the way the barn was set into the ground, the whole south-facing long side was open. That side of the barn had a barnyard, too: a nice, flat area bound by a beautiful stone wall. Since it was empty, we could let Dansin live down there, so I set up a smaller enclosure inside one of the sliding doors. We could leave the doors open, and he could go in whenever he wanted, or stay out. That fall and winter, he was a free-range horse, going into his roomy stall-sized area when he felt like it, meandering around the big yard when the mood took him. There was a staircase from the first floor to the cellar, so I could easily bring him his hay and grain without even going outside. It seemed to work well.

That winter was typical: some snowstorms, some sunny days, cold, yes, but warm breaks, too. Every time I'd check on him, Dansin was either standing around resting, or walking slowly, perfect rehab for the tendon. He was completely relaxed, and when he was outside, he could watch people riding by. One day, after we'd had a few inches of snow, I drove up and looked down into the yard. He was standing by the gate idly watching a pair of riders coming down the road. I looked again: there, on one half of the yard, there was a big circle of packed-down snow. Hah! Even though no one ever saw him running around or acting nervous, at some point his compulsion kicked in, and he'd slowly circle. The proof was right there in the packed-down circle of snow: he was stall walking even without a stall!.

When his leg looked tight, we brought him back to the track. As a four-year old, he was content to be there, and trained well, but things just didn't seem to go his way. There were few races that really suited him. If he could have a race on the turf, it rained. We realized, too, that he was much better at longer distances and the races that came up for him were all too short. I used to say that if Nijinsky himself had had to race in Boston, he'd have died a maiden. Dansin's stall walking was manageable. The combination of his friend Jerry, tied at the front of his stall, and an arrangement of hanging boards and ropes kept him from going full-tilt. He ran a total of twelve times, and had two third places – not a fantastic record, but any income at all helped defray the expenses of the horses on the farm. In May, we all had a real adventure: there was a race at Belmont Park that seemed to suit him, and it just so happened that Marian Manning and Bob Hindy were driving down with one of her brother's horses, too. Their owner had his own van, and they invited us to take Dansin along with them. It was too good to refuse.

The day arrived. Bob, Marian and I would ride in the van with the horses, and Jim would drive down and meet us there. We'd all stay overnight, race the next day, and return. A reasonable plan. Dansin and I loaded up early in the morning. He marched right on the van, and seemed to get along well with his travel mate. Jerry, too, went along, and the assortment of boards and ropes that were Dansin's stall furniture. Bob drove, and Marian and I sat up front with him.

All was well until we stopped for gas in Long Island. We were a little lost, but got directions; and when we started up, the truck was dead. This was not funny. Stranded in Long Island with two horses and a goat. There was a crowd gathering around, looking at Jerry peering over the door of the van, and they looked a little too interested. Just when I was about to panic, Bob noticed that the battery had become unattached; he fixed it – and we were on our way. Soon, we were driving in the stable gate at Belmont. There was someone walking out as we pulled in – Eddie Sweat, the famous groom of Secretariat! I was convinced that this was a positive sign.

Being at Belmont Park was overwhelming in itself: the home-bred, home-trained Dansin breathing the same air as the best horses (and trainers) in the country! We settled the horses into their stalls and rigged up Dansin's anti-walking equipment. It was late afternoon, and still light, so I brought Dansin and Jerry out to sample the grass under some trees. As Dansin was grazing, a Mercedes drove by, and I noticed the driver was the legendary Woody Stevens. He looked over, stopped, backed up, rolled his window down and I stopped breathing. The great Woody Stevens noticing my horse! He leaned out the window, looked at me, and said, "Good lookin' goat!"

That may have been the high point of the trip. We settled the horses in and went off to find the hotel. The next morning, I was so nervous I couldn't eat breakfast, anxious to get back and check on the horses. When we drove up to the barn, there was Dansin peering out, bald-faced. When I walked over, he and Jerry greeted me and I stopped. The stall had a track worn right through the bedding, and his halter was dangling from the rope I'd tied him to. He had managed to get loose from his tethers, and had spent the night doing what he did best.

Just being at Belmont with our homebred was a thrill in itself, though. Jim took pictures of Dansin in their famous paddock, walking by the bronze statue of Secretariat. The race itself unfolded as expected, but Dansin, worn out from spending a night stall walking, lacked his usual late run. He didn't embarrass himself; he finished in the pack but we were disappointed.

When the turf season came to a close, we brought him home. During the summer, the farm had decided to increase the number of boarders, and they'd put new stalls in the ground floor. Dansin lost his winter quarters. There was a small building on the other side of the barn, though with a paddock. At some point, it had held chickens; and in later years, one of the pony stallions. Linda Cunningham, Woody's assistant and resident carpenter, adapted the little building to make a run-in shed for him, so he once again was a free-range horse for the winter. This paddock was on the cold side of the barn, and right in the path of the winds that came barreling across the big front field, but there was another paddock adjacent to this one, separated by a chain-link fence, and there were horses there for company. I bought him a pricey turn-out blanket, thinking that would help him weather the coldest days, but the very first time I put it on, I returned at the end of the day to find him standing patiently at the gate, dressed in nothing but a very attractive surcingle, the blanket in shreds all around him. He seemed oblivious to weather: one day, in the middle of a raging sleet storm, I drove up to find him standing in his shed, with his whole head and neck sticking out the door. His mane and forelock were covered with ice, his eyes were shut, and he was sound asleep, a blissful smile on his lips. In the early spring, mud season, he looked like a yak: his thick winter coat layered in mud, dried to adobe, but as the days warmed, his thick hair shed, the mud fell off in hunks, and his spring coat shone forth, a metallic, gleaming bay, better than all the boarders' horses who'd been coddled inside all winter.

Now he was five. When he returned to Suffolk, I was assigned stalls in barn C, on the sunny side. We had our two two-year olds there, too, and a horse I was training for other people. I was still trying to figure out a solution to his stall walking: the goat/hanging board/ tether system worked fairly well, but it wasn't ideal. I had had an interesting conversation with a psychiatrist I'd met at Saratoga, who dealt with stereotypic behavior in humans. He said studies had shown that mental patients did better when their rooms were painted pink, so, leaving no stone unturned, I bought a gallon of paint and covered the walls of his stall. The result was, well, not exactly restful. The pink was more like Pepto-Bismol but he seemed to like it. The goat did, too. Did it stop the stall-walking? Of course not.

One weekend, I was working in a stall when I heard voices: a crowd of people was walking down the shedrow, led by Becca Woods, who worked for the track publicity. As they neared, I heard her voice. "And now, this is what we call a stall-walker. Notice the goat, the pink walls, the hanging board" Oh, terrific! Now he was on the Saturday stable tour.

He's Dansin "Al Fresco" with Sinbad the cat at Suffolk.

The stall-walking was taking its toll on me, too. I'd send him to the track first, and after he'd cooled out, I'd tie him outside to the grain shack between barns, with a haynet and some water, and leave him out there until the last possible minute before I had to leave. He was completely relaxed out there, and one day I had the thought: Why don't we just let him live out there? I talked to Steve Pini, who was the head of track maintenance: Could I build a stall-sized enclosure beside the grain shack, out of the lanes between barns, and leave him there? Steve was agreeable, so the next day, I arrived with lumber: four posts, and boards for the side. I already had a stall screen for a door, and we put a large piece of plywood on the roof of the shack, jutting out as an overhang. I brought a post-hole digger from the farm, but we found out very quickly that the ground was so hard-packed that it was useless. Jim ended up digging out holes for the posts by hand, using one of the hand-forged hoof picks the blacksmiths made.

It took most of the day to finish this project and the people working in the barn probably thought we'd lost our minds, but when we were done, I filled the area with shavings and turned Dansin loose, with Jerry tied right by the door. He had a healthy roll, shook himself off, and went right to his haynet. A few hours later, he lay down and took a nap, flat-out in the afternoon sun. I dismantled all the lines and boards from his stall and stored them on the grain shack roof; they may still be there to this day.

The outside stall was a huge success. Immediately, he started gaining weight and his work on the track was much more energetic. We did fine-tune things: I bought a colorful beach umbrella, and when we had a sudden downpour, he'd stand under it to escape the rain. The barn cat Sinbad took a shine to the whole setup, and he'd often lie on the plywood overhang, shaded by the umbrella, his tail drooping down. Dansin was dedicated to rolling, so we had to add kickboards around the perimeter to keep his shavings contained. One day, the local news channel showed up, and that night he had a five-minute bit on television.

His career as a five year old was difficult. It was still hard to find races on the turf with a distance that suited him. He did have a few seconds and thirds, but no wins until the Mass Breeders program was expanding, and they added a new stakes race: the Boston Common Stakes, seven and a half furlongs on the turf. There were a few horses in the race who were proven: Tonight's the Night, who had won multiple stakes, and Isadorable, who dominated the Mass Bred fillies and mares. Still, this was our big chance. Norman Mercier agreed to ride him. Norman had had a long, distinguished career, and was enthusiastic about riding him on the turf course. Once again, I spent the whole morning of the race obsessing about the weather, doing a reverse-rain dance.

The Boston Common! The race attracted a good crowd of onlookers; the paddock was full of owners and trainers and breeders and friends. Dansin was his usual debonair self, good to saddle, relaxed in the warm up and gate and then, "They're off!" Once again, he broke alertly, but the second stride out of the gate, he was trailing. Around the first turn, he looked like he was competing with the outrider behind the field. Down the backside, he was running, but still many lengths behind. Then, the final turn. Coming out of the turn, I thought he was gaining on the outside, and then as they came down the stretch, I realized he could be fourth! No, third! No, second! He was suddenly moving faster than everyone else, and I could hear Jim Hannon, the track announcer: "And as they come to the wire, it's Tonight's the Night and He's Dansin is FLYING out here!" He'd won!

Cathy Chumbley escorts Norman Mercier and Dansin to the post.

That year, he ran eleven times in all. The highlight was the stakes win, of course; but late in the fall, he ran in the Columbus Day Handicap, a wide-open race, and finished a closing fourth. His running style, coming from way behind, going very long on grass was not suited for the races they were running at Suffolk at that time, but he made us proud. Living outside made a huge difference, too; after training or racing, he'd go back into his outdoor stall, have a nice roll, and take a nap in the sunshine.

Late in the fall, friends suggested we enter him in a race at the Meadowlands. They said the turf course was beautiful; the race was long and would really suit him. Foolishly, we agreed. We sent him down in a C&W van with Rick Dolan, as groom, and we flew down. I am about as far from a "frequent flyer" as they come, so I was paralyzed with nerves. Going through the security check, I set off the alarm: I had his bridle and metal bit in my purse. Then, my seat on the plane was broken. When we got there, we hailed a cab and told him to take us to the Meadowlands. The driver took us to the nearest phone booth and called a friend for directions! When we finally got to the barn area, we did find Dansin, but no sign of Rick. He was playing cards in another barn. Then, since Dansin was a Lasix horse, we had to take him to the Lasix barn until his race. Right away, I knew this was a mistake: it was an enormous airplane-hangar kind of building, and the stalls had wooden floors, with televisions posted throughout, piping loud race coverage. The result was deafening noise and confusion: no place to have a stall-walker. The only way to keep him relaxed was to hold him, so I stood in his stall with him for the three hours before the race, patting his neck and talking to him until Jim looked at me with horror and said my nose was bleeding. Sure enough, I had my first (and last) major nosebleed!

The race itself was an anticlimax. We were sure that after all that, he wouldn't run well, and he didn't. Again, he didn't disgrace himself, but he lacked the closing rush that had become his trademark. We loaded him on the van for home, and started looking for a cab to take us to our hotel. Wimpy, the van driver, offered to drive us himself, so we all – Wimpy, Rick, Jim, me, Dansin and Jerry – drove right up to the front door of the hotel in the big horse van. Wimpy dropped us off, and drove off to Boston with Rick and Dansin and Jerry looking out the door. The look on the doorman's face was almost worth the whole trip. The next morning, we flew back to Boston. As the plane dropped down for a landing, we realized that the flight pattern would take us right over the track. Sure enough, we looked down and saw the track, the grandstand, all the barns, and there, lying flat out in the sun, in his private patio, was Dansin!

After that, it was home for the winter. Once again, he spent his time out in the elements, grew a huge, mud-caked winter coat, and then sloughed it off in the spring to reveal a shiny bay underneath. When it was time to return to the track, he dragged me up the ramp of the van, anxious to get back to his Suffolk home.

Dansin genuinely enjoyed being a race horse. He trained well, and all morning, stood in his sunny outdoor stall watching other horses being walked, bathed, hosed and then had a long nap. He got lots of attention from people walking by; life there was never dull. As a six-year old, he ran a total of six times. Once again, it was hard finding races long enough, and when we did, they were very tough. Then, in the fall, the Mass Breeders put on another turf race, the Autumn Turf Handicap. This time, the rider was Rudy Baez. Rudy was a very successful rider, and a local favorite. For that reason, it was hard to get him; but he was available for this race. I didn't need to explain anything to him; he knew Dansin by being on the backside in the morning, and he'd seen him run. He was confident, and we were hopeful. The race turned out to be a complete surprise. We expected the usual performance: break well, then drop back and amble along until the final turn, and then make a run down the stretch. Not quite. He broke well, but going down the backstretch, he was roaring by horses. He went into the final turn with the leaders, and coming around to the head of the stretch, he left them in the dust. He coasted by us and under the wire with the rest of the field fighting for second place.

That year, he went home to a hero's welcome. Most of the boarders at the farm didn't have much interest in our racing enterprise, but when we drove up to the barn with a big silver trophy, they were amazed.

He did go back to the track as a seven-year old. He was happy to be there, but the old injury to his tendon was starting to bother me. The exercise rider claimed he felt fine, but I was always scrutinizing it: is it larger? Is it growing? I was constantly asking the vet to check on it. Dansin ran five times. His best performance was in another running of the Boston Common stakes, where he ran fourth, beaten by horses that he'd toyed with the other time. The last time he ran, we ran him for a claiming price, trying to give him easier competition. Jose Caraballo was his rider, and we couldn't fault how he rode him. He was relaxed in the post parade, broke well, willingly traveled along until the final turn. I was standing at the front of the paddock watching as they turned for home, expecting to see him accelerate. He didn't; he kept running at the same speed he'd run throughout. I knew as he crossed the wire that this wasn't good, and sure enough, when he galloped out around the far turn and pulled up, Jose jumped off.

This was a nightmare moment. How many times had I dreamed of some disaster, a horse injuring himself in a race and riding home in the ambulance? I started running, racing down the track toward Dansin standing by the gate. I saw Dr. O'Gorman's jeep speed over, and suddenly felt like I was in slow motion. What if someone had claimed him, and had him put down? I couldn't stop that. What if he was broken beyond repair? Dr. O'Gorman was wonderful: he knew I'd bred him myself, and knew how much he meant to us, so he smiled encouragingly as I ran up. "He'll be fine, we'll give him a ride home. He's reinjured that tendon."

Dansin was standing quietly. Jose had already taken off his saddle and was climbing into the jeep for a ride back to the jock's room; the horse ambulance was pulling up. I loaded him myself; he walked right up the ramp with his usual aplomb, and I rode back with him. The ambulance drove right along the outside fence, right past the grandstand, and as I was standing inside, I could look out the back door and see the crowd staring at us. When we passed the pony people sitting on their horses by the paddock, Cathy Chumbly looked in at me, then turned and yelled to the crowd, "He must be okay. She's got a smile on her face!"

It was a smile of pure relief. He was not okay, but he would be. As soon as he was able to travel, he went home to his chicken coop and the paddock with a view.

He's Dansin: 37 starts/ 3 Wins (two stakes wins) / 1 second / 4 thirds

Pee Wee Valentine and He's Dansin in the paddock for his first race.
Vernon Bush in the "Schoolbus Farm" silks!

                    HE'S DANSIN
    Owner   Suffolk Downs   7.1/2 Furlongs
    School House Farm   J.Vargas
    Trainer   2nd.Dancing Spring   Time 1:38.1
    Susan Walsh   3rd.Brazen Romeo   May 29, 1983

```
              "The Boston Common Stakes"
                HE'S DANSIN          $22,500 Added
Owner           Suffolk Downs        7 1/2 Furlongs
School House Farm   Turf             Norman Mercier
Trainer         2nd.Tonights The Night   Time 1:36.4
Susan Walsh     3rd.Flip For Ross    June 23,1985
```

Aggie and Duly

Duly Royal (Duly) and Agatha C. (Aggie)

Even though we'd decided early in our program to resist the temptation to breed our mare back after she foaled, we were accumulating horses faster than income. Fortunately, Mother Nature gave us a break. We bred Tenny back the year after she foaled Dansin, but it didn't take. Now, we were going to breed her back again. I had joined forces with a group of fellow breeders to form the Massachusetts Thoroughbred Breeders Association, and one of our members acquired a new stallion, Great Mystery, and syndicated him. I couldn't resist; I bought a share. He was standing at Kimball Farm in Pepperell, an hour away. I loved the farm; it was owned by the unforgettable Louise Kimball, who was one of our original board members, too. Her farm was wonderful: an old New England setting, with something interesting going on at all times. When Great Mystery arrived, she built a special stall just for him, and all of us sent mares to him.

That first year, Tenny's date with him was fruitless; now, we were going to try again. Again, I hitched up my trailer and set out. When I was leaving the farm, one of the boarders volunteered to ride along: Mrs. Potter. Her daughter had a pony at the farm, and they lived nearby, so she would appear every morning to turn the pony out and relax in the barn door with her coffee. She was a wonderful woman, and by that time in the spring, had become a good friend, so I welcomed the company. Then, as we were leaving, Lane McIntosh ran up and asked if he could come. Lane's father had rented the front house, and even though they weren't horse owners, Lane and his brother were always around the barn, playing with cats, talking to the boarders, helping me feed the carrots. Betty Potter and I welcomed him, too.

Tenny was good about trailering, and good about breeding. It was always easy to tell when she was in heat, so I'd told Louise that she might very well be receptive. When we arrived, Louise came out to watch her unload, Mrs. Potter wandered off to look at Louise's beautiful garden, and Lane scampered off to pat the barn cats. Louise and I took Tenny down to Great Mystery's stall, and he came right over and put his head over the door.

Tenny acted quite interested; he acted even more so so Louise said, "Well, let's try it right now." Her capable manager came over, Great Mystery came out in all his glory, Tenny looked coyly over her shoulder, and the two got together. Just as their date was reaching its thunderous climax, so to speak, I noticed that Lane had come out of the barn where the cats were and was standing wide-eyed at the door. I thought maybe this might be a little too much animal magnetism for an eight year old boy, but…

The pairing seemed to be a success. Midge, Louise's manager, settled Tenny in her stall, and they said they'd repeat all that until she went out of heat. So far, so good.

Mrs. Potter rounded up Lane, and the three of us headed back home, Mrs. Potter and I chatting away in the front seat, while Lane sat silently behind us. After a half hour or so, his voice piped up: "Susan, when you breed Tenny again, can I come with you?"

This was not our only breeding this year. After watching how much easier it was to raise foals with other foals, we had decided that we should have another mare. John Burke had claimed a mare the previous fall he'd sell us. His friend and confidant, Joe Salah, a student of pedigrees and conformation, thought this mare had all the attributes for a good broodmare, so sight unseen, we bought her. I drove down to Suffolk to pick her up, along with my friend Mrs. Potter. When we got to the barn, no one was around, so I walked down the shedrow looking for the new mare. I walked all the way to the end and back and finally realized that the strapping big bay that I'd thought was a gelding was our new horse. She was very handsome, and seemed sensible and gentle. We led her out to the trailer without incident, and she rode back to the farm without moving. This could be good.

When we got to the farm, all the boarders who were there clustered around to see the new horse, and I proudly went to back her off. Well, she couldn't. Her hind end seemed frozen, and then her hind legs would jerk up spasmodically. Finally, she semi-turned in the trailer and semi-fell back into the barnyard. This was amazing: here was a horse who'd won a race a few weeks before, and now she couldn't back up. How courageous she must be!

This mare, Royal Stand, was born in the same year as Millie, but what a difference. Millie looked like a horse who'd never been used; this mare had an enormous right ankle which was almost frozen, and this odd neurological glitch in her hind end, yet she was the one who'd won multiple races.

Jim came by in a few minutes to view our latest addition. He liked her right away; loved her size, and her commanding presence. He also thought her gentle and wise, so he decided that henceforth she'd be known simply as Lady.

Now, this spring, we were going to breed her, too. We were pleased with the results of our sending Tenny to Maryland to be bred; we loved Lady's breeding, and decided to send her to Maryland, too. Again, the stallion we chose was a young horse who had accomplishments as a racehorse, but was standing for the first time, so his stud fee was reasonable. While Tenny went off to Pepperell in my trailer, Royal Stand (Lady) shipped in a big C&W van to Maryland to be bred to Due Diligence.

Our operation was growing fast. We had an official stable name for this enterprise: Schoolhouse Farm, a tribute to the fact that we lived in the old schoolhouse out back. We had our own silks: dark green, with a lime green sash and lime stripes on the sleeves. We had now bred three horses who had all made it into training, and by the time we bred these two mares, two of those foals were winners. It was amazing to us that we could follow this dream from our little rented house, on a farm where we rented space by the stall, and end up competing with breeders and owners of all levels. When Millie was training at Rockingham, we went to Saratoga for a few days, and one afternoon I walked toward the paddock and spotted the legendary Penny Tweedy walking in the same direction. Millie's sire, Millstone, was by Brian G, a stallion who stood at Meadow Stud, Mrs. Tweedy's Virginia farm.

I couldn't resist. "Mrs. Tweedy! We have a granddaughter of Brian G in training at Rockingham!"

The great lady stopped, looked me right in the eye, smiled, and wished me good luck. I felt like a teenager at the stage door. What a wonderful sport this was!

Now, as the spring deepened, my life was wilder than ever. John Burke had urged me to take out my trainer's license, after working for five years as a groom. I did, and now I was training Pete before school, getting up at dawn and driving to Suffolk Downs, then racing over to Cambridge to teach, then racing home to deal with the horses there. Dansin was getting ready to go to the track, too, which would make things even more complicated and now, we were on the foal watch for two mares: Tenny, working on her fourth foal, and Lady, with her first.

Lady was fast becoming our favorite. She was so quiet and calm, so gentle with Jim, that "Lady" really suited her. She was very rickety: an enormous front ankle that was virtually locked, and that odd neurological glitch in her hind end. It bothered us more than it did her, however. She was always eager to go out, and was a good companion for Tenny. She was great to work with, and came when she was called. She was, in short, absolutely no trouble.

Her pregnancy seemed to be on course. The extra weight didn't seem to affect her soundness the way we'd feared, and her appetite was good. When her udder started to fill, we moved her to the stud barn, so that she could foal in a roomy stall, in a barn that was more peaceful than the big barn, with its constant stream of boarders. So, the nightly checks began.

Since this was her first foal, she wasn't devious about it at all. She had an almost textbook foaling: udder filling up, then waxing up and that night, she went into labor. I had checked on her before it started, and as I puttered around in the barn she showed signs of discomfort. Soon, that turned into labor. When it intensified, she lay down in the deep straw, and didn't mind it when I slipped in and crouched behind her. More labor; more contractions. Suddenly, the appearance of a foot, then a leg, then another, then a nose. Again, I grabbed the legs and applied just a little traction with her contractions and, whoosh! Once again, we'd gone in a flash from two to three. Lady immediately relaxed; I pulled the caul over the foal's head. The foal raised her head, wobbly on its short neck, and flailed around with her front legs. Then, the hind legs. Then, the rustling of the straw drew Lady's attention. Sure enough, that moment I'd come to love: the mare sees the foal, her eyes bulge, the foal nickers, and the mare summons a voice she'd never used before in reply.

Once again, I felt the flood of emotion: excitement, of course, looking at this brand-new member of our herd, and relief, that the long wait was over, and the foal seemed healthy and alert. After a few minutes, I ran home and told Jim, and then we stood in the aisle and just watched. The foal was, in fact, a filly. We determined that, and dealt with the navel and the afterbirth. Then we looked closer. She was cute obviously, but also compact – almost chunky. She didn't have the long legs Pete had, or the long pasterns we'd seen in Millie; or the sleekness of Dansin. She was a fuzzy grayish brown, and feisty. She hopped to her feet with a minimum of gawkiness, and was small enough to figure out how to nurse without having to twist her head under the mare and up to the udder. She could just walk over and reach up. She seemed to adapt to life in the outside world very quickly, and she was friendly, too. Even just hours old, she'd walk right up to us and stare into our eyes. With her coloring and chunky little mane, she looked like a burro. She was, in fact, special. Jim went to work on a name, calling upon the sire (Due Diligence) and the dam (Royal Stand) to produce "Duly Royal." To us, though, she was forever Duly.

Lady carried her calm, gentle nature into motherhood: she was a perfect broodmare. The next day, we turned them both out into the small paddock right outside their door, and Lady hovered around her new baby, of course, but she wasn't obsessive. The foal romped around in the sun, dashing in little spurts away from Lady and then back. I noticed watching her that she didn't seem to put her left hind flat on the ground. When she stopped, it was always cocked. Jim noticed it, too. What to do? We did what we always did: waited. After two days of her frolicking around, the slight contraction in her tendon that caused that had gone; she was perfect!

For four days, their world was that small paddock. I came home late that fourth day and first went to bring Tenny in from the pasture; then, when she was settled in her stall in the main barn, I decided to go play with Lady's foal. As I left Tenny, I mentioned to one of the boarders that it looked like she was getting close to foaling. I thought she'd start to wax up at any time. I went over to the stud barn and brought Lady and her foal in, gave Lady some hay, and stood in the stall with the foal, who seemed to love attention. Suddenly, one of the boarders came in, nervous and excited: "You'd better come look at Tenny. She's lying down and acting funny."

Oh, great! I ran over to the big barn. It was right in the middle of feed time, so the farm helpers were rolling the feed cart in the aisle. A few boarders were brushing their horses in the aisle, too. The music was blaring, and most of the horses in the barn were making that "hurry up and feed" noise. It was pretty chaotic. I ran to Tenny's stall: sure enough, she was lying down and there was a leg jutting out from under her tail. We had straw on hand for her foaling, but we had been waiting for her to wax up before bedding the stall. I quickly opened a bale, and strew it around while she groaned and moaned. I barely had the stall bedded when the foal dove into the world onto the fresh straw. So much for the serenity of the stud barn late at night. Everyone there was peering into the stall watching as the foal struggled to her feet.

Another filly. This one was a beauty: a very feminine head with a nice star, long legs, a light, golden bay. She looked correct conformationally, too and like little Duly, seemed alert and healthy. In the next stall, Majorca was nickering. Somehow, he must have known that this was another project for him. Tenny couldn't have been more relaxed. She let the foal nurse, then went right to her feed tub. Foal number four was in the building! When Jim drove home from work, he was greeted by a foal who looked like she'd been around for a week, doing everything right. We were stunned: no sleepless night for this one!

In five days' time, we had increased our horse herd by two. As we had hoped, having two mares with foals made life easier than having an only child. Lady and Tenny were both relaxed mothers; they got along famously, too. The two fillies took to each other immediately, and while the mares grazed, they played. As spring turned into summer, the sight of the two foals racing around the field drew everyone's attention. We loved watching them. Tenny's foal, who was by Great Mystery, now had a name: Agatha C. Aggie and Duly spent their days running together and resting together. Often, tired out by all their running, the two would plop down in the grass side by side.

Aggie and Duly.

As they grew, they developed two distinct styles. Aggie was all grace. She'd walk into the pasture, pick up a gentle trot, extend it, and slip into a canter. She'd make big sweeping circles, switch leads gracefully, and change directions in flowing figure-eight's. Duly? She would rip right into a gallop, squeal, buck, and zig-zag crazily, all the time making noises that sounded like "leaving rubber." We'd call her the car wreck. We suspected that Aggie had a great future; we just loved Duly, period.

We found that having two mares made weaning easier, too. When the time came, we took Lady away one morning, and Duly and Aggie went out with Tenny. Then, three days later, we whisked Tenny away, leaving the two buddies in the care of Majorca. Aggie knew him as the friendly horse in the next stall, and the three of them got along famously. With Majorca on guard, we never worried about them. They'd spend long days in the pasture, racing each other around under his care.

Majorca was getting old. He'd developed navicular problems, so I'd long since retired him from riding. Now, as the fall turned into winter, I thought he'd need a little extra protection from the wind and the cold. We have never been dedicated to blanketing our horses; we let the foals grow nice fur coats for the winter, and they all seemed fine. Still, I had to protect my aging noble steed, so I bought a New Zeland rug. Those wonderful blankets were heavy green canvas with thick wool felt linings. They weighed as much as a small pony, but were impervious to rain and wind. Plus, they made Majorca look quite spiffy. One raw day in November, I sent him out with his "girls" dressed in this finery, and went off to work. That afternoon, I drove up to the farm, and I could see Majorca standing in the middle of the field in his new green coat. He looked, well, sheepish: the two foals were standing behind him, grabbing the skirts of the blanket and lifting it up while they peered underneath. Eventually, they got used to it and the teasing stopped.

Duly and Aggie had a wonderful childhood, playing together in their nice big pasture with Majorca standing by. The winter was no problem for them, nor the spring. Then, in late summer, it was time to get them "broke." I started them up the way I'd done for the others: tacking them in the stall to get used to that, then teaching them to lunge in the round pen, then longlining. They were both fine. Meanwhile, I had Pete and Dansin in training at the track, so I didn't have a lot of time to spare. My exercise rider at that time was Mark Perry, and his wife-to-be, Eileen, helped me get the horses out in the morning before school. I mentioned that I was getting ready to get on the two yearlings, and Mark volunteered to help. He'd started his riding career breaking yearlings at Norman Hall's stable in Norfolk, and had always enjoyed it, expressing the same nostalgia that John Rodger had. We agreed that he and Eileen would come to the farm for a week, after I got home from school, and we'd get the two girls started.

Duly & Aggie learning the ropes with Mark Perry.

We did just that. The first day, Mark and I took them one at a time into the round pen, tacked up. I did a little long-lining with them, and then he got on. No problem with either one. The next day, we repeated that – and then he rode each into the big ring. Again, no problem. For the rest of the week, we took them together. He had Duly; I had Aggie. We jogged them around the big ring side by side, then cantered, then did the same thing the other way. The two of them loved it. Jim took pictures of us, all smiles, and that was our Christmas card that year. After that week, we declared them "broke" and they went back to their carefree childhood.

When they turned two, it was time to get them ready for the track. At this point, I was still teaching, still running to the track and training before school, still busy beyond my wildest dreams. The farm was busy, too. There were now boarders everywhere, filling not only the main floor of the barn, but eight new stalls downstairs, and even a few in the stud barn. If it was daylight, there was someone riding in the ring, someone lunging in the round pen, and people tacking up in the aisle. We decided to send the two "girls" to Norman Hall's farm to get fit for the racetrack. I had become good friends with Norman; we were both founding directors of the Mass Breeders, and his son John, who ran the farm, was a good friend, too. Mark Perry was thrilled that I'd decided to do that. They had a good training track, competent people, and a great reputation. The horses went out in sets of two, and got a great foundation for galloping at the track.

The years had not been kind to my trusty trailer. "Trusty" had become "rusty." It was now a repository for odds and ends from the track, unsafe at any speed. I turned to my old friend Joe Moore. I had met him when Millie was at the track as a two-year old, when he was John's assistant (He still kidded me about replacing the watch she'd smashed). Since then, he'd gone into the horse transport business, and had a very nice six horse trailer, so I decided to send the fillies off in luxury.

We sent Duly off first. I hadn't done any trailer practice with her at all, but Joe wasn't concerned. He set up a box stall for her, and said that in his experience, if a horse rode in a box stall, he settled down much better. He was absolutely correct: she left the farm without looking back and arrived at Hall's without incident. We were another matter; we had become very fond of this funny little filly and we missed her terribly. Aggie looked lost out in the field with Majorca. We told John we'd give her time to settle in, but would visit in a week or so.

Saturday, we set out for Norfolk. We arrived mid-morning, parked on the street, and walked over to the barn. It was a huge, old New England bank barn, its front end right on the road, and the ground floor accessible from the back. We walked down the sloping drive beside the barn, looking over to the training track to the right, and just as we reached the back of the barn, two horses came out heading to train. There she was! One of the two was our beloved Duly. Someone had pulled her mane, and I remarked at how mature she looked with the new haircut. We called to her as they rode by, but she didn't respond. We were both sad about that, crushed at how fast she'd forgotten us. "Wow! She doesn't know us!" I cried. Then, just as I said that, a familiar whinny came floating out from the depths of the barn. The horse we'd seen wasn't Duly at all; she was still inside, and she'd heard my voice.

Amazingly, the horse we'd first seen did look just like her: a plain bay filly with no markings. Duly herself was sporting a strange blue halter. Somehow her halter had been mixed up with another. It made her look a little different, but there was no denying who she was. By the time we'd patted her to death, the two horses had returned from the track, and she went out with a companion. This time, she looked right at us as she walked by. She was all business on the track, seeming to relish galloping with a companion, and when she returned, she immediately morphed back into our funny little child.

It wasn't long before she was ready to go to the track, and when she left Norman Hall's, Aggie took her place. When Aggie had done her work there, she joined Duly at the track. I had my hands full. We now had four horses of our own in training at Suffolk Downs. I had another one, too: a handsome colt I was training for four New Hampshire owners.

Duly and Aggie, born just days apart, spent their childhood together and now they started their careers together, too. They both settled into the racetrack routine quickly. They liked the activity in the barn, and enjoyed galloping on the soft cushion of the racetrack.

Aggie was very easy to deal with, and obedient under saddle. Duly ended up staying at Hall's longer than I'd planned. She contracted a guttural pouch infection, and the vets advised working through that before sending her into the track. Ultimately, though, they were both in my barn, in adjacent stalls. Since Dansin was installed in his outdoor room, Duly inherited the Pepto-Bismol stall. She could look right out her stall door and watch Dansin picking at his hay net or sleeping in the sun.

"The Terrible Two's" did not apply to these two. They both enjoyed their gallops all summer, and gradually progressed in their training. When they were babies, Aggie seemed the more mature, but now that they were actually at the track, it was Duly who seemed to grasp her new career. Aggie was well behaved, but didn't seem to have that tenacious competitive streak that Duly showed. Both of them trained regularly. They avoided shin problems, and Duly actually ran twice as a two year old, something very unusual for our horses. Granted, it was late in the year (both races were in December) but she did. Then, in February, she won.

Henry Ma was in the irons for that exciting event. He'd ridden Pete, of course (and won on him), and was a reliable, trusted rider. He was very tall, at that time probably the tallest jockey in the colony, and we always joked about his win on Duly (who was chunky but short-necked) that his nose may have been in front of hers at the wire.

Duly in the pink "Pepto Bismol" stall.

Duly turned out to be one of our best. She was not a large horse, but she was stout, and she had a genuine love of racing. I was always concerned about her feet. Even as a foal, her hooves were not the typical shape: they looked like little hockey pucks. Her stride wasn't the classical one, either; she always looked choppy galloping. She had an enormous heart, though and relished the competition. The feet were her weak point. She was fine on the deep winter track, but when the spring came and the track tightened up, it took its toll. We finally got into a routine of giving her the summer off, waiting for the fall and the deeper track. She stayed in training though; and galloped all summer; but we backed off on breezing and racing.

One day, she was in a late race, and the clouds rolled in early in the morning. By the time we had to bring her to the paddock, the track was the proverbial "sea of slop." As we walked up, wading through the wet, I thought to myself, "Why are we doing this to her?" Well, when the gates opened, that question was answered: she loved it! She opened up a healthy lead immediately, and sailed around the turn and down to the wire with her ears pricked. Rudy Baez rode her only once, but again, it was a sloppy track, and she won. As he pulled up, he said, "She just played with those fillies!"

Jose Caraballo won several races on her, as did her particular favorite, Bill Klinke. When I run into people to this day, when they reminisce about her, they always add Bill Klinke's name to their memory.

She ran in a simple D-bit, one with little copper rollers. One of her races was particularly memorable. The horses loaded into the gate, the gates opened and she won. As Billy jogged over to us, he yelled, "How do you like the bridle?" I did a double-take: it was a bright yellow nylon one. What??? When they were loading, an assistant starter had grabbed her reins to lead her into the gate, and her bit snapped in two, dangling uselessly out of her mouth, so they had to grab their spare bridle, make a quick change, and load her. We thought, of course, of what would have happened if the bit broke during her warm-up, or even worse, during the race but we will never forget that day.

We were thrilled with her progress. She was shod with leather pads to baby her strange feet and the blacksmith would simply cut out the pads the day of her race. That seemed to work well, until one time when she was running on a Sunday. My blacksmith was nowhere to be found! I walked down to Bill Perry's barn, hoping that his blacksmith was in his usual spot there. He'd taken the day off, too. When I explained why I needed him, Bill went into his tack room, came back out with the proper tools, and followed me down to our barn and performed the operation himself. He was our leading trainer, with a full barn of horses, but he still took the time to do that simple favor for me. We never forgot! She won that day, too, so the following day I delivered a bottle of wine to his barn.

All her wins had been sprints. One time, we tried to see if she'd like to "go long." That day, just as we were walking to the paddock, the fog came rolling off the ocean, and by the time her race went off, the visibility was limited to the stretch. Larry Collmus was our announcer at the time, and with his usual wit and aplomb, he made the best of the fact that you couldn't see most of the race. Finally, the field emerged from the fog at the eighth pole, and we looked frantically for her. The rest of the horses flashed by, and then, at a discreet distance, in a genteel slow gallop, there she came. Billy Klinke's comment as he pulled up, "She doesn't like going long."

Duly's last start, with Stewart Elliott, escorted by Charlie Aro & his pony.

Duly endeared herself to many people. She was feisty on the track, but when she walked into the paddock and stood in the stall to be saddled, she was eerily calm. There was a popular coffee commercial at the time featuring Juan Valdez and his burro. The way she stood there, so quiet and meek, reminded us of that, so we started calling her Dule the Mule, a nickname everyone picked up on. For years after she'd stopped racing, people would stop me in the grandstand and ask if I still had her. She was a tough competitor. If the conditions were suitable for her, you could bet on her giving her best – and many people did just that.

Most of her races were at Suffolk Downs. In 1989, the owner of the track announced that the track would close at the end of the year. She won a race that December on one of the last days. The owner had not winterized the track, so that day, a cold one, the surface was like powder, not normally to her liking. She won the race, though, and the Chairman of the Racing Commission was there himself, overseeing what everyone thought were the final days of racing, so, I prevailed upon him to get in our win picture.

Shortly after that, everyone from Suffolk relocated to Rockingham, in the dead of winter. Normally, Rockingham ran in the summer, when she had her time off, but she ran seven times there as a seven-year old. Finally, that spring, we decided she'd done enough. In her last race, she missed winning by a whisker. Stewart Elliott was her jockey.

Duly Royal: 58 races / 10 wins / 8 seconds / 6 thirds

```
                      DULY ROYAL
Owner                 Suffolk Downs        6.Furlongs
SchoolHouse Farm                           Henry Ma
Trainer               2nd.Mene Wishes      Time 1:16.1
Susan Walsh           3rd.Agil Girl        Feb. 3,1986
```

DULY ROYAL

Owner	Suffolk Downs	6.Furlongs
Schoolhouse Farm		William Klinke
Trainer	2nd.Light Brown	Time 1:13.3
Susan Walsh	3rd.Easter Lullaby	Sept.24,1986

```
                        DULY ROYAL
Owner                   Suffolk Downs              6.Furlongs
Schoolhouse Farm                                   William Klinke
Trainer                 2nd.London Valentine       Time 1:14.2
Susan Walsh             3rd.My Twoloves            Oct. 17,1986
```

	DULY ROYAL	
Owner	Suffolk Downs	6.Furlongs
Schoolhouse Farm		Jose Caraballo
Trainer	2nd.Lady Carlton	Time 1:12.4
Susan Walsh	3rd.Arrive on Time	Sept.6,1987

	DULY ROYAL	
Owner	Suffolk Downs	6.Furlongs
School House Farm		Jose Caraballo
Trainer	2nd.Cardinal Flower	Time 1:13
Susan Walsh	3rd.Sweet n Joyful	Sept.20,1987

```
                        DULY ROYAL
Owner              Suffolk Downs         6.Furlongs
Schoolhouse Farm                         William Klinke
Trainer            2nd.Miss Throttle Wide  Time 1:15.1
Susan Walsh        3rd.Single Kiss       Feb.1,1989
```

```
                    DULY ROYAL
Owner               Suffolk Downs          6.Furlongs
Schoolhouse Farm                           William Klinke
Trainer             2nd.Grecian Day        Time 1:12.3
Susan Walsh         3rd.Warm Spot          March 3,1989
```

```
                        DULY ROYAL
Owner               Suffolk Downs              6.Furlongs
School House Farm                              Rodolfo Baez
Trainer             2nd.Make It Memory         Time 1:13.4
Susan Walsh         3rd.Real Moody             April 17,1989
```

```
                        DULY ROYAL
Owner                   Suffolk Downs           6.Furlongs
School House Farm                               William Klinke
Trainer                 2nd.Lucy's Great Love   Time 1:13.4
Susan Walsh             3rd.Rose Of The Forest  April 29,1989
```

```
                       DULY ROYAL
Owner              Suffolk Downs                6.Furlongs
School House Farm                               William Klinke
Trainer            2nd.Red Top Delight          Time 1:14.4
Susan Walsh        3rd.Sueno Switch             Dec.15,1989
```

As thrilling as Duly's career was, Aggie's was disappointing and puzzling.

As a foal, she was beautifully built, and graceful to watch. At the track, she was well behaved and willing, and looked elegant galloping. She was not a big horse, but she was very pretty, with a sweet face and a disposition to match. She was easy to deal with at the barn and obedient to gallop. Everything should have been fine, but there was some indefinable ingredient missing.

Aggie and Duly.

Her training went well; she went through all the motions without a problem. She never bucked her shins, never got sick, never got sour-but she also never seemed to grasp why she was there. It was as if she'd been born with the brain of a Golden Retriever instead of a race horse.

She didn't run at two; and she never ran at three, either. There was no particular stumbling block in her training, but she just never progressed to where we felt she was ready. Finally, as a four year old, I entered her. We picked the easiest race we could; we didn't want to overmatch her. The day arrived. She walked willingly to the paddock, stood obediently for the rider, warmed up nicely, and walked into the gate without hesitation. She broke with the rest of the field, and then found a comfortable cruising speed. We watched patiently, waiting for her to ramp it up, to begin a move on the backside, to start passing horses - and it never happened. She was on cruise control. The field came around the turn and headed to the wire, she cruised at the rear. The field crossed the wire, galloped out, pulled up and she continued, on cruise control, around the turn, down the backstretch, still on that steady pace, until the outrider had to go catch her and bring her back.

The worst part of that dismal performance was that she didn't seem to realize how bad it was. She walked back to the barn as cheerful as ever, cooled out normally, and went right to her hay.

We thought maybe she'd learn from that experience, so we entered her again. Again, she hit a comfortable cruising speed and maintained it throughout the race, after the race, and again, until the outrider caught her. Well, maybe she'd prefer a longer race. We tried that, with the same results. Maybe she'd prefer the turf. Wrong again.

This was puzzling. She was the fourth foal out of our mare Tenny and the other three had all won. One of them, Dansin, had won stakes races. Nature vs. Nurture? She was raised right alongside Duly, who had already won several times. I looked for a physical explanation. She did have a habit of resting with one of her front legs forward. I nagged our patient vet, Marty Simensen, trying to find a reason for her dismal performance. Carol Dudley, who shared a barn with us and had even galloped her, sat around with me for many hours theorizing about what was missing. Finally, we resigned ourselves with the thought that her talents lay elsewhere.

AGATHA C: 10 Starts / no placings

Penance (The Rodent)

We had an enforced gap in our foaling: we did breed the mares the year after Duly and Aggie were born, but they didn't take. Just as well; we now had eight horses in one stage or another, and the farm was getting more and more crowded. Still, I had that share in Great Mystery and Millie was just occupying space. We had stopped racing her when Pete started. She did win one race, but that was her third start, and once she'd realized what her life as a racehorse was, she became more and more fractious: nasty in the barn area, rank in the paddock, violent in the gate. Then, when the gates opened, she'd just tear away to get clear and then pack it in. She didn't have the competitive racehorse mentality at all. I had turned her into my riding horse for a while, riding around the farm, taking her places with my friend Nancy and her horse Supie, but now I didn't have the time for it, with my teaching and training. She was athletic, though, and hale and hearty.

We sent her to Great Mystery, and it took. Then, to help ease our budget, my sister, Jeanne, who lived south of Boston, agreed to keep her for us. She and her two daughters loved horses, and they had a small shed behind their house. Her husband, Larry Taylor, built a nice paddock for her, so down she went.

When the time came for her to foal, we were in a quandary. Foaling her out at my sister's wasn't an option; foaling at the farm at this point, with people fighting for turnout time and keeping the barns busy well after dark wasn't a good plan, either. I had become friendly with a woman who was a new member of the Mass. Breeders, and she had a very nice small farm: immaculate pastures, brand-new barn, and other mares in foal, and she was eager to have more business. I thought that would work, so when the time arrived, Millie went over there to Alice Foote.

The farm was perfect and the foal would have companions, which was good but this was the first time I wouldn't be there. Still, Alice was competent, and frankly, I was so busy with all the other horses that we felt it was a good decision, so that spring, Millie foaled without my help.

Alice called to tell us she'd had a beautiful bay colt. Everything had gone fine, although Millie was her usual dramatic self. In a few days, I had the time to go visit, and was pleased. Physically, the foal was fine. He was getting along famously with another foal, and they had all day in a nice pasture with good fencing. Now, the name. Jim focused on the Sin of Sin Mill, and came up with "Penance." That was fine with the Jockey Club, so Penance it was.

I was focusing all my energy on the horses under my care, leaving Alice to worry about him, and things went smoothly until, of course, they didn't. Alice called with the news: they were bringing the horses in for the night, and Millie was impatient. She was standing at the gate having a little hissy fit, waiting to go to the barn, and when Penance walked around in front of her, she bit him. Not a motherly little nip, but a serious bite. She took quite a hunk out of his hind end. The vet was called, of course, and treated the injury, but it was a setback. Alice and her daughter were meticulous in their care, covering the wound when he was out during the day and keeping it clean. I went down to check, of course, and she had not exaggerated. He had a large piece of muscle missing. It was healing well, though, and it ultimately did – but left a large, unsightly scar. Well, I quoted old Dr. Orcutt, "a long way from his heart," and hoped that it would turn out to be unsightly but irrelevant.

After he was weaned, a stall opened up at home, so we brought him back. He spent the next year at home, and I got to know him. He was a friendly little guy, with some endearing habits: he loved picking up sticks and carrying them around, amusing himself most of the day. We gradually stopped worrying about his ugly scar; it didn't seem to bother him at all.

When he turned two, it was time to consider breaking him. Again, the farm was so busy, as was I, that I couldn't see where I'd find the time to do it myself. At one of our breeders' meetings, I talked with one of my colleagues, and he mentioned a woman who did all their breaking for them.

She had a place not fifteen minutes from us, so I called, liked what I saw, and sent him over. It was a hunter/jumper barn with an indoor ring. She and her daughter had broken many Thoroughbreds, and had no problem with him. I thought, too, that if his race career didn't work out, he'd have a good foundation for a riding horse.

His education went without a hitch. I went one day to observe, and was thrilled with how well they'd schooled him, so off he went to the track, foal number six. This was the only foal I hadn't hovered around from birth to "graduation" to the track. When he left for the track, the woman who'd worked with him said diplomatically that she hoped I didn't have high hopes for him, but I'd learned that you could never predict how these babies would do until they actually did it, so I got a stall ready for him at Suffolk Downs, and he joined my little herd there.

Penance at Suffolk Downs.

Of all the foals we raised, I felt the least connection with this handsome little bay. He was Millie's first foal, but since our farm was getting so chaotic with all the boarders, he was born at a friend's farm, and moved to another farm, the Ryans, until he was a yearling. He was back with us through the fall and winter, and then in the spring of his two-year old year, he went to get broke and from there, right to my barn at the track.

I had four other horses at the track at the time, and his stall was on the backside of theirs. He was a congenial sort, and his early training had been solid, so he started off with the same routine all the young horses go through: going to the track every morning and galloping.

When he'd been a younger horse, at the Ryans' Farm, he'd acquired the nickname "The Rodent," since they said he'd run around his paddock, nose to the ground, poking at whatever he found there, "like a little chipmunk." Hence, The Rodent. Of course, that unflattering nickname followed him. He was mentally active, true: when he was in his stall at the track, he was always looking out over the webbings and following the goings-on. When he was on the track himself, he was just as curious. This made for some fairly hair-raising gallops, when he'd sometimes careen around, reacting to something he'd seen. Fortunately, I had George Trenger as his exercise rider. George had worked for many years at Norman Hall's stable, and there weren't many horse gymnastics he hadn't encountered. He was as unflappable as The Rodent was reactive. They made an interesting pair.

Life went on. He trained, getting more and more fit, adapting to the track routine and his neighbors in the barn. He seemed tireless: he'd gallop on the track, cool out quickly, and then go back to his stall for a nap. His version of a nap was lying flat-out in his stall, but sticking his whole head and neck under the webbings right in to the middle of the aisle and leaving his eyes open, watching the activities in the shedrow at ground level. Needless to say, someone stepping into the barn and seeing a horse head on the ground tended to be unnerved.

He seemed sound. He did have a horrible scar on his hindquarters which he'd acquired as a foal, but that didn't seem to bother him. He had good feet, good wind, and a good attitude. Slowly but surely, he reached enough fitness that I considered letting him breeze. There was nothing about his training yet that made us concerned. Now we just had to see if he had the desire to be competitive.

One day, I followed him to the track and stood at the eighth pole to watch. We just wanted him to breeze a quarter-mile, basically just down the stretch. He cantered onto the track, then galloped by me down and around the first turn, then down the backside. It was late in the morning, so there wasn't a lot to distract him, and he approached the quarter pole moving well. He passed the quarter pole, still moving well. George changed his hold, urging him on but there was no acceleration. He was still moving well, but nothing seemed to change. Maybe his feet were moving a little faster, maybe there was some difference, but I couldn't see it. When they came back to the barn, George concurred. He asked for more speed, he got nothing.

A few days later, we tried again. He galloped off willingly, looked fine going down the backside, but when he was supposed to shift gears, nothing.

I felt a flashback to Aggie. Was this another clueless horse? All these weeks of training, building up his fitness for this? I consulted my long-suffering veterinarian, Marty Simensen. Marty, the consummate professional, gave him a long, serious look. He watched him jog in the road, he watched him walk toward and away from him, circle on both directions, back up. He put his all-knowing hands on him, moving his legs, flexing his joints. He stood outside the barn, right elbow cupped in his left hand, pondering this equine enigma. He x-rayed his stifle.

Marty's conclusion: he wasn't hitting that fifth gear that racehorses have, because he couldn't. The injury to his hind end he'd received as a foal, with all that scar tissue, had made his stifle joint unstable. He didn't have the muscling there to allow the engagement needed to go from gallop to run. So, was Penance my penance, payback for breeding a one-win, bad-attitude mare in the first place? I finally decided it was just bad luck. He could walk/trot/canter with the best of them, but running was not in his future. Of all the horses we'd bred, his racing career was the shortest.

Penance: unraced

Sunny Reign (Reign)

Fortunately for our budget, once again nature gave us an enforced break in our breeding. We tried breeding Lady back the year after she had Duly, but it didn't take. Then, we sent her to Maryland on a foal-sharing agreement. She had a foal which they kept, and the plan was that they return her to us in foal. Well, she wasn't. We had quite a gap in our master plan. We'd leased out Tenny to a friend who did get a foal from her but we were foal-less. That didn't mean that we were horse-less, though. The handsome colt I'd trained for some people from New Hampshire had injured himself. The owners sent him to another trainer, where the injury became career-ending. They then contacted me, hoping I could find a buyer for him. Well, the injury precluded a career as a riding horse, so, in one of my moments of horse-madness, I volunteered to take him as a stallion. Just what every one-mare farm needs, her own stallion!

Sunny Clips! I had bought him as an unraced two year old for my owners. He was bred in Florida, and I thought he was wonderful: a bright chestnut with three white socks and a Golden Retriever disposition. The day he arrived at the track, my vet, Marty Simensen, looked him over with his practiced eye, and declared: "There is no such thing as perfect, but this colt comes pretty close!" When he raced, he was just as impressive. He won three races in a short period of time, and showed speed and intelligence. He had interesting breeding, too. He was by a son of In Reality, and thus a direct descendant of Man O' War. My owners, who were new to race horse ownership, were ecstatic. Then, the injury, which seemed minor at first; but his career was cut short. Now I thought he deserved a new life as a stallion.

Right before he was to come home, Woody, the farm manager, approached me. After thinking about my bringing Sunny home, he thought it would not be wise to have a stallion at the farm now, with all the boarders. I was stunned. There was the stud barn, and there were still pony stallions there. I was at a loss for an alternate plan, but my good friend Pat Dudley had an idea. She knew a woman who had a small private farm who'd be willing to board a stud. Sure enough, she was agreeable. The farm was quiet, with good turnout and solid fences, and an easy ten-minute drive from home, so Sunny moved right in.

What an amazing business. In a few short years our idea of raising a race horse had ramped up to where we would now raise foals from the minute of their conception. A daunting thought.

When it was time to breed Lady, I wanted to make sure that Sunny got off to a good start as a stallion. I didn't want him to become a rank, unmanageable stud, so I consulted an expert: Pete Bundy. Pete was a lifetime horseman. He'd been in the cavalry in World War II (he sounded not unlike General Patton, actually; and lived in Hamilton), and now he managed the stallions for a prominent warmblood breeder in his home town. He was also the Department of Agriculture man who worked with the Mass. Breeders, so we were friends. He quickly agreed to handle Sunny for his first "date," and show me a routine I could follow when I handled him. On the appointed day, Lady and I trailered over to meet Sunny. Pete met us there, and took right over. I brought my friend Dan Winning, who worked at the farm, as moral support.

Lady's ladylike temperament made it difficult to tell definitively when she was receptive to be bred. That day, I was fairly sure she was, and had showed her to one of the more aggressive geldings at the farm. She didn't object, so we put her in the trusty trailer and headed over.

While Dan waited outside with Lady, Pete and I went into the barn and he prepared Sunny for the task ahead. Pete was firm with him, made him stand when he asked, and cleaned him up. Then we brought him out and he and Lady were introduced. Fortunately, she was in a receptive mood and, even though he'd never done this before, Sunny soon figured it out. The day was a success.

Two days later, Dan and I repeated the procedure by ourselves. This time, he held Lady and I went in and brought out Sunny. Sunny was more excited, knowing what was ahead but he was still manageable. Again, it was a success.

When she went out of heat, we held our breaths for two weeks, but she came into season again. Back to the trailer-to-Sunny routine. Dan and I were getting good at this: we could hitch the trailer, load her, drive over, and unload her and be ready to breed in a half hour.

That cycle went by, and she was back in again. I almost gave up. It was getting late in the spring, and this would be a late foal. One morning, I was talking to Dr. Sheehan at the track and bemoaning the loss of a whole season, because now it would be a late foal. He looked at me and said, "Better a late foal than no foal!" So, back again. I checked Lady at home, and thought she was still breedable, so I called Dan, but couldn't locate him. This was before the day when everyone carried a cell phone. I called his house, and no one answered. I started to panic, sure that this would be the last chance to catch her on this cycle, and just then Jim drove up. Reluctantly, he agreed to be a stand-in.

Off we went to Sunny's farm. When we got there, I brought Lady over to the spot we'd been using, and drew a line in the dirt. I told Jim to hold her right there, with her front feet on the line, then went back and brought Sunny out of the barn. Sunny on a calm day was an imposing horse: tall, with a big muscular body and a commanding presence. On a day when romance was in the air, he was stunning. When I led him out of the barn, head high, nostrils flared, feet dancing with excitement, Jim blanched. He had never seen a live breeding before, and he was standing right on the goal line. We approached Lady, who stood her ground, nice and relaxed, and Sunny took a flying leap and threw himself on her back, his front legs over her shoulders. This meant, of course, that his front hoofs were just a few feet away from Jim. Again, Jim blanched. "This could be dangerous!" he said, but to his credit, he stood his ground.

After that date, Lady never seemed to come into season, so in a few weeks, we had her ultrasounded, and she was pronounced in foal. Jim was convinced that it was his handling that did it.

The next spring, Lady's due date approached. Every birth was exciting to us, of course, but this one had special meaning, since it was the first foal for Sunny. If this foal turned out to be a winner, it would mean a lot for his career as a stallion.

It had been five years since Lady had had her first foal, Duly. That had gone very well, but in those five years, a lot had changed. The farm was even busier than ever, with boarders around constantly. All the ponies had gone: it was all boarders now. In the yard behind the stud barn, there was a row of horse trailers. Mine paled by comparison with the new models lined up there.

Lady was five years older, too, her tricky hind end was worse, and she had come back from Maryland with her bad ankle even larger than before, so we were concerned about making her comfortable. Woody suggested that we let her foal in what the boarders called the dungeon stall. It was a large windowless room on the ground floor of the barn, originally a root cellar. It was accessible by a staircase leading down from the first-floor tack room, and a door leading out to the barnyard. It was also, as its nickname suggested, pretty gloomy. It was quiet, though, and roomy. We cleaned it all out, and filled the whole room with fresh straw. There was a source of water right there, and an old wooden manger from the days when the calves would winter there. We opened the door to the outside, a wooden door which we could swing up and hook to the ceiling, and after a day of airing out, the room looked much brighter. I put up a stall screen in the doorway so Lady could stick her head out, and we moved her in. She actually seemed to like it there, so we decided that it would work as a maternity stall.

Now, the watch began. Once again, I monitored her udder. Once again, it filled. Then one afternoon when I brought her in from the pasture, she was waxed up. Once again, I started the nightly checks. We no longer lived in the schoolhouse. They had reclaimed it for a pre-school, so we had asked permission to fix up the milk room of the old, vacant dairy barn. Now, we were living there. It was a perfect small house for us and it was also closer to the barns. From our bedroom window, I could look over and see the top of the door to her stall, so the night checks were considerably easier. I could go in the main floor of the barn, slip into the tack room, tiptoe down the stairs, and look through the small window to see Lady without even disturbing her.

I did the nightly check. Then, the next night, and the next, and the next. Now we were getting worried. She had waxed up, and now she was running milk. This could be a problem. I suspected that she was fully aware this time that she was about to foal, and was waiting for us to let her alone. Finally, on the fifth night, I snuck over and tiptoed down the stairs, peered in, and eureka! She was pacing around, sweat glistening on her neck. I felt that initial wave of panic (Wait! Let's wait a minute!) but then slipped into the stall just as her water broke. What a wonderful mare. She strained, of course, but was so stoic about it that the only sound was the rustling of the straw. Then, again, the appearance of our next hope, in a rush. Lady knew immediately what she'd done: no shock of recognition, just the mother-to-foal nicker, the voice she never used except to her foals. The foal was a beauty, too. I hadn't thought about color, but she was all her sire, a brilliant chestnut. A beautiful symmetrical star, a lovely feminine face, and long, long legs. When she got to her feet, she was stunning.

Everything seemed perfect. Lady's reactions were wonderful, the foal's instincts were great, she looked healthy. I was concerned, though, that Lady had run milk for so many days. Had the foal been able to get the vital colostrum? The next day, we called the vet to come and check her out. This time, the Orcutts sent their new vet, Brian Parrot. I had never met him before. He was new to their practice but he was confident in his assessment. He recommended that she be give plasma to compensate for the loss of colostrum.

Give the foal plasma: simple, right? This involved laying her down in the straw and running IVs. I was very thankful that Lady had such a benign disposition, and glad that this was not her first foal. She was, as usual, wonderful. We let her stand around without restraint, and we lay the foal down in the straw. Now, naturally, the foal's first instinct was to get up, so I had to kneel down beside her and make sure she didn't, while Dr. Parrot rigged up the IVs. Amazingly, everything went perfectly. The foal did let me hold her down. Lady stood patiently by observing, and the IVs ran without incident. It did seem to take forever, though, and at one point I mentioned that if anyone happened to look in, they'd have to wonder why I was lying face-down in the straw next to some handsome young guy.

When Dr. Parrot had finished, I let the foal scramble to her feet. She stood in the straw shuddering, but he said that was just her body adjusting to the plasma. Sure enough, after a few minutes, she went over to Lady for a drink, and right back to her role as beautiful, perfect foal. Well, almost perfect. When she was stable and we got a chance to look closely at her, we noticed she was "windswept." When you stood behind her and looked at her hind end, her hocks both blew off to the left, like a gust of wind was hitting them broadside. This bothered us, of course, but after a day or so being out in the pasture, she strengthened, and self-corrected.

She ended up having a wonderful childhood. There was a long stretch of idyllic spring weather, which turned into wonderful summer weather, and she had long lazy days in the pasture. We were back to the only-foal mode, which we'd hoped to avoid, but Lady was so relaxed that the days passed easily. When it was time to wean her, once again Majorca stepped up. It was love at first sight. She took to her new companion without a backward glance.

Jim came up with her official name: Sunny Reign, a nice combination of Sunny Clips and Royal Stand, and she was known henceforth as Reign. We moved her back upstairs in the big barn after she was weaned, in the stall next to Majorca and once again, the hole between the two stalls was their gathering place. Majorca was turning into our secret weapon in foal raising. He genuinely loved foals, was patient with them, and very protective. The two of them went through the winter without incident. The next year, she had grown into a stunning yearling, so I was tempted to bring her to the yearling show. The old Yankee Thoroughbred Breeders had disbanded, after the closing of Rockingham Park. Suffolk Downs was now the only track in New England, so our new organization, the Massachusetts Thoroughbred Breeders Association, began hosting yearling shows. Our founding

Chairman, Linda Ramsey, drummed up a lot of enthusiasm for the event, and brought in judges from the "outside world." It was tempting to show Reign, but I was caught up with helping in the production myself, so she stayed on the farm.

The only cloud on her horizon came in late fall of her yearling year. It was an average day. I'd come home from teaching, messed around at the barn, and had brought her in for the night. I was at home that evening finishing up the dishes, when one of the boarders came to the door. Apparently, Majorca was lying down in his stall and acting odd. I threw on my boots and rushed over.

Majorca was down. He was quiet, not thrashing or sweating, but not right. He had a vacant tuned-out look in his eyes that gave me an ominous feeling. I put a call in for the vet. He had had a bout of colic a few years before which had scared me; I had a call in for the vet that time, too, and he was in obvious pain. I was outside leading him slowly around in the dark when the vet's car turned in at the drive. Then, he raised his head, whinnied, let out a blast of gas, and promptly recovered. By the time the vet parked the car, he was his old self.

This time was different. It was the vacant look in his eyes that scared me, as if he'd given up. In the last few years, his life had become routine. I had long since stopped riding him and his only job now was mentoring the foals. He was now twenty-five, "long in the tooth," and starting to look his age, but up until that night, he was always himself.

The vet arrived, and it was Dr. Parrot once again. He evaluated him quickly, and feared the worst. He did a peritoneal tap and confirmed it: there was a rupture somewhere. I didn't have time to panic. We quietly led him to a discreet corner of the barnyard, and, as Woody would say, "Lay him to rest." I was glad that he had had little time to suffer, glad that he'd been his old self right up until that last night, but it took a long time to adjust to life without the trusty steed who'd been right there when I needed him for twenty years. The next morning, Reign went out as usual but without Majorca, which was so hard to see. I waited until there were horses in the adjacent pasture to give her company and she didn't race around frantically but she kept looking for him all day. So sad!

Sunny Reign learning her trade on the farm. My easiest pupil!

Spring of her two-year old year. It was time to get her under saddle. I thought I'd send her off somewhere, the way we'd done with Duly and Aggie, but I'd start her off here. I did the preliminaries. She had no problem being tacked up, and one afternoon when the barn was unusually quiet, I put the tack on and led her to the back of the main aisle where there were some hay bales stacked against the wall. I climbed up on them, then leaned over the saddle. She didn't mind. Then, I swung up and sat on her. Again, she didn't mind, so we walked down the aisle. It only took a few steps for her to get used to my weight, but once again, it didn't bother her at all.

After a few days of that, I got on her and let her walk to the pasture while I was sitting on her. Again, she didn't mind, and when we got there, I untacked her and turned her out. That went on for a few days, and then I was making a circuit of the ring, then another, and before I knew it, I was settling her into a routine. For a while, just walking; then I began jogging her, then cantering, and before I knew it, she was broke to be ridden. I didn't want her to get sour before she even got to the track, so I kept things short, and always ended with turning her out. Then, one day Beverly Hardcastle, who was working at the farm, had her horse saddled when I was doing this, so we rode together. Her horse, Cardiac Arrest, was a wonderful, rock-steady quarter horse who had actually been a pony at the track. Reign seemed to like the company, and the next thing I knew, we were walking out of the ring and up the back road. Reign was interested in the change of scene, but stayed nice and relaxed. One day, we rode past Sunny in his paddock, father and daughter eyeing each other over the fence. I wanted to keep things at a low key. I didn't plan to send her to the track until I was out of school for the summer, so I'd get on her and amble around for ten or fifteen minutes or so every day. I also didn't want to tell Jim, fearing that he'd want to step things up. One afternoon, I came home from school, brought her in from the pasture, put the tack on her, and rode up the back road. Just as I was riding toward our house, I saw his car in the driveway, and as we walked by, I spotted him by the side of the house, mouth agape. We were caught.

Reign turned out to be amazingly amenable to whatever I came up with. My old trailer was way too decrepit to use any more, but I thought she should have at least some schooling in that area so one day I hitched it up and parked in the yard. I dropped the ramp and led her over. She stopped, looked inside, and then, when I walked in ahead and called her, just strolled in after me. So, without even planning to, I had her all broke and track-ready by myself.

When school was out for the summer, it was time for her to go to the track. This time of year, it was Rockingham, just a ten minute drive away, so I called C&W horse transport, and they sent their horse van over. The van was much different than a trailer: the ramp was much steeper, and the van was huge. Nevertheless, when I walked on, she followed right behind. She arrived at the racetrack ready to go on with her training, without ever hitting a snag of any kind.

Reign was the opposite of Penance. I'd rarely had a horse that I was more involved with. From the minute she was born, I was just about the only one who touched her. I'd done all the breaking myself. I hadn't planned to, but it just turned out that way. I got her fit enough on the farm that she went from there right to the track. We were at Rockingham now. Duly had been there until mid-spring, when we decided to breed her, so Reign took her place.

Even though I had had not a moment of trouble with her, I knew that Reign was so used to me alone that being handled by anyone else would be a hard adjustment, but as luck would have it, I found a terrific exercise rider who understood my concerns. Edna Sargeant! She was about my size, albeit much slimmer, and could ride "long" if needed. She also agreed to start off mounting the way I did, standing on a bucket. Reign's introduction to someone new went pretty well. I wasn't riding her, but I was still her handler, and I always walked her to the track and back.

Reign adjusted to the track very well. She got along well with Edna, and like most other young horses, found the open space of the racetrack and the flow of horses interesting. She learned the routine quickly; the only snag at first was that a friend of mine, Richard Trimmer, had a pickup truck identical to mine, and since her stall faced the back road, when he drove by she'd see the truck and start hollering.

Spring turned to summer, and her training progressed right on schedule. Finally, I decided it was time to get her used to the starting gate. She'd been so good for so long that we went to the track as usual, and I stood at the gap where I always did. This would be her first stop at the gate, and all she'd probably do was walk through with the doors open, so I didn't go with her.

I watched her gallop down the stretch, around the far turn, pull up and jog behind the gate, and waited for a few minutes. Then a few more minutes. Then more. Now, I got nervous; just walking through the gate shouldn't have taken long. Finally, I could see her galloping away at a nice pace. She went by me looking fine, went down the stretch, pulled up and jogged back. As Edna jogged toward me and walked off the track, however, she shook her head, and her face had a serious look. She filled me in: it had not gone well. Reign went behind the gate calmly enough, but one of the starters walked up to her and grabbed her bridle, which startled her, and then when he tried to lead her toward the open stall, she balked. Things escalated rapidly and it finally turned into quite a battle. This was not the introduction to the gate that we'd wanted.

RESOLVED: Never again would I do so much hands-on myself. From now on, our horse would be exposed to as many different people as possible. "Cut the cord," as my mother would say.

Reign had been at the track for weeks now, and hadn't hit a snag, but this was definitely a snag, and it was a big one. Horses had to be good in the gate, period. After we let her settle down for a few days, I tried it again. We'd go to the gate for a walk-through, but this time, I'd go with her. I borrowed a bike, and as Edna galloped around the front side, I peddled frantically down the back road. My plan was to stand by the gate, out of sight of Reign, but just be there.

The starter was Tom Schwigen, one of the best in the business, but I'd never met him. Duly had run there many times, but she was already seasoned, and I'd never had the opportunity to go to the gate in the morning. Now, as I stood at what I thought was a discreet distance, he called over. "Hey! Don't be hidin' over there! Come up here where I can see you!" I sheepishly crossed the track and walked over to Tom, standing by the side of the gate. "Now look," he cried, staring at me with hawk eyes, "This may be your little darlin', but this filly ain't worth two dead flies if she don't learn how to get in that gate without a fuss." That was just the beginning: he delivered a rant at me that would have humbled D Wayne himself. I didn't say a word.

Reign came up a few minutes later, and thank God she was smart enough to know it wasn't worth fighting. She was hesitant at first, and he was hard on her. I thought that probably he wouldn't have been that tough if I hadn't been standing right there. She walked up, froze, put her nose toward the gate, backed up and then one of the starters looked over at me and said, "Oh, don't worry; she'll be fine." He was still looking right at me, put his hand on her hindquarters and her leg shot out and hit him right in the knee. This wasn't good. Two other starters carried him off, Tom's fierce expression tightened up a notch, and I wished I'd never borrowed that bike.

Somehow, they did manage to get her to walk through, and I promised I'd bring her back soon. When we got back to the barn and she'd cooled out, I staggered to the kitchen for a cup of coffee, wishing it were Irish. As I sat there trying to forget the whole ordeal, Grady, one of the starters, came over. He was so kind that I almost teared up. He told me not to worry, the man she'd kicked was fine, Tom was just a perfectionist and he'd personally take care of her the next time she came over.

Grady was as good as his word. Every time we went to the gate, he'd come over, take Reign's bridle, talk to her, cajole her and eventually she accepted the process. I wanted her to go over there, go in, go out and go home, but Tom, rightly so, knew that in the afternoon it was never that quick, and they had to learn to tolerate the confines of the stall as long as necessary. It seemed like whenever she went to the gate, she was there for hours.

Now she was starting to breeze, and one day we sent her to the gate with a jockey, Joe Hampshire. Tom made her wait, then once in, made her stand, and stand and finally let her go. Back at the barn, I was feeling picked on, so when John Burke came by I ranted to him. John was no longer training. He was Joe's agent, and had come by to find out how the work had gone.

"Well, it was fine, except that what's-his-name, Wiley Coyote guy kept her behind the gate forever," I fumed. The next time she went to the gate, this time to get her "gate card," I borrowed the bike again and pedaled over to let Tom know we wanted to go for her card. He saw me coming, and came over with the smallest of smiles. "So! I guess you think I look like that Wiley who??" Mortified once again I silently cursed the borrowed bike but Tom did have the decency to smile and Reign got her gate card.

That snag was finally resolved (and she turned out to be well-behaved in the gate for the rest of her career), but then we hit another: she started tying up. I'd never had a horse of mine tie up, although I'd seen plenty of others. She didn't seem to fit the mold, either: she wasn't a nervous horse, she wasn't unfit, but now it was a nightmare. She'd gallop fine, and then as she came back to the barn, usually when she was steps away from walking into the shedrow, she'd start shortening stride and breaking into a sweat. I tried untacking her as she walked; we tried having the rider loosen the girth. I had a new exercise rider (since her original exercise rider, Edna, had left), Chris McKenzie, who got along famously with her, yet she'd still tie up. One day, I asked Dave Lezell to gallop her. Dave was more than competent. He was the outrider at Suffolk, and was as calm as the Marlboro Man on horseback. He sat motionless in the saddle. I thought he'd be able to let her relax.

The day he galloped her, they set off as usual, and I couldn't help but notice what a nice pair they made. Dave so tall and slim, and Reign a beautiful, poised mare, well over sixteen hands. They looked wonderful galloping by, too, but as he came jogging home, I could see her shorten stride and she tied up so badly that he had to pull up and dismount before they were even off the track.

Once again, I turned to our wonderful vet, Marty Simensen, for answers. Marty had just taken on another vet in his practice, the talented Mary Kahn, and he had her research the whole problem, looking for answers, but it was a long, frustrating battle. Any change in the track surface would trigger an episode.

Like Dansin's stall walking, Reign's tying up consumed me. While I was coping with the episodes and trying to get her through it, her training did go on. She trained all winter, dodging tying up episodes and winter storms, and then, little by little, through the spring, she progressed, until finally she made her debut.

Joe Hampshire rode her that first time. She started slowly, but made a good run at the end and gave us hope. She didn't tie up after the race. For some reason, tying up seemed to be rare in horses in an actual race. For her second race, Joe was committed to another horse, so we teamed her up with Billy Klinke, who'd had such success with Duly, her older sister. Billy rode her three times at Rockingham that year. By the time she'd made her fifth and final start as a three-year old, it was December.

Sunny Reign, and Robbie Holman, in the paddock at Suffolk.

The next year, Suffolk reopened after a two-year hiatus, and Reign, now a four-year old, started her career there brilliantly. Ridden by our friend Jose Caraballo, she won a race in January, another in February, and a third in March. Now, we thought we were getting somewhere. My teaching job was ending and after a twenty-five year stint, I was being phased out when the school downsized, but having a horse who was winning so easily and so often made me cavalier: So what? I can make a living training!

Well, that didn't go well either. Reign, after looking so brilliant, tailed off. She seemed to lack power and I noticed she walked lop-sided. Again, I drove my vets to the brink, asking them to watch her jog, floating theories about her poor performance. Mary thought she was getting a knee. We x-rayed it, and nothing showed, but she thought the problem might be cartilage. We actually sent her to Tufts for possible arthroscopic surgery. When we got there, Dr. Kirker-Head took her into the aisle and examined her. He did the standard jog-toward-him and jog-away and then he did the same again, first flexing each leg. I held her front legs in turn and she jogged fine. I held up a hind leg and jogged her and I was stunned. She almost fell, then lurched down the aisle like a wounded duck. The arthroscopic surgery was tabled, and she went instead for spinal x-rays. His conclusion: kissing spines.

Kissing spines! What could we do about this? We backed off on her training, and Mary did injections right between the spinal processes involved. We gave her more time off, then brought her back very carefully. In the spring, we decided to run her on the turf. We'd run her on the turf at Rockingham and she hadn't done well, but the Suffolk turf was different, and we thought turf would be easier on her hind end.

Sunny Reign in the Winner's Circle at Suffolk
with Robbie Holman and Jose Caraballo.

Jose Caraballo was riding her once again. I was nervous, but Jim was excited, looking forward to seeing her on the turf. Robby Holman, my friend who always ran her for me, was dubious. Robbie and I stood at the edge of the paddock as the race went off. It was a long race, so the gate was on the frontside. She broke well, as she usually did, and then the field swept by. She was right there, striding out, moving gracefully over the grass. Jim came running over, yelling: "She loves it!" Robby agreed that she looked the part.

We watched eagerly as the horses ran down the backside, but when they came to the far turn, she seemed to flatten out. The energy had gone from her stride and she came by us almost eased. When Jose rode her back to us, he was somber. "She felt great for a while, but then she just fizzled."

Her story was like so many others: obstacles to overcome, a period of hope, and even a run of success, but finally, one obstacle too many. That fall, we brought her home.

Sunny Reign: 15 starts / 3 wins / 2 seconds

```
                        SUNNY REIGN
OWNER                   SUFFOLK DOWNS          6.FURLONGS
SCHOOL HOUSE FARM                         JOSE C. CARABALLO
TRAINER                 2ND.CRIMSON BARBI      TIME 1:14.3
SUSAN WALSH             3RD.PASS THE CAVIAR    JAN. 29,1992
```

	SUNNY REIGN	
OWNER	SUFFOLK DOWNS	1 MILE
SCHOOL HOUSE FARM		JOSE C. CARABALLO
TRAINER	2ND. TAB'S STAR	TIME 1:47.2
SUSAN WALSH	3RD. QUEEN OF SOUTH	FEB. 24, 1992

Sunny Clips looking at his first foal Sunny Reign.

Sunny Crime (O2B)

When Reign was born, we stuck to our determination to resist breeding the mare back, even though we had an in-house stallion now. We had bred Sunny to Lady so many times by now to produce his first foal, Sunny Reign, that it felt more like a marriage than a mating. Love was in the air, though and since Millie was available, we decided to breed her. Yes, she'd had that moment of rage when she bit her first foal, but we were hoping that was an isolated incident.

The farm where I initially had Sunny had closed, so we sent him to Oakhurst Farm, owned by the Ryan family. They were wonderful horsemen, and had lots of experience not only with mares and foals, but with stallions. When Millie came into heat, we sent her there. I was busy with school and the track, and my trailer was now a lawn ornament, but I saw the Ryans every day at the track, and could keep in touch.

In due time Millie was declared in foal; now a year later her due date was approaching. As with her first foal, I was leaving this to the experts. One night, I had a strange dream: I was at a farm, not ours, but obviously a farm, and someone said that Sunny had fallen into the well. I ran over to a hole in the ground and looked in: it was a wide, stone-lined hole, glistening with water, and way down below was a horse's head, a chestnut with a blaze. In the dream, I reached down and grabbed his front hooves and pulled, and he floated up to me, then glided out onto the lawn. Strange! That morning, I went to the track, then school and I was teaching a class when a colleague said I had a phone call. It was my vet, Erica Fuller, calling to tell me that Millie had foaled, a chestnut colt with a blaze!

After school, I drove down to Ryan's farm to see our latest foal. Millie was still in the foaling stall with him, and was in one of her rages. Erica had wanted to get in and check the foal out, but Millie was having no part of it. Fortunately, Millie recognized me. I was able to grab her, and Erica and her partner Sue Montgomery gave the foal a good examination. They pronounced him "beautiful." He did look just like his father. He looked like Millie too, of course, chestnut with a blaze, but even as a tiny foal, he had his father's powerful build.

For the next six months, Millie and her foal lived at Oakhurst Farm. Early on, he got sick and ended up battling pneumonia. Erica and Sue were right on top of it, though. Sue even made nighttime visits to give him his meds and pull him through. He was so sick for a while, though, that the Ryans started calling him "Otta Be," for "Otta be Dead." Well, he survived, took his medicine, and then prospered. I was still so busy that I made only the occasional visit, but I was impressed with his handsome looks. Jim once again came up with an official name for this son of Sin Mill and Sunny Clips: Sunny Crime. The Jockey Club accepted it, but the nickname, O2B, stuck.

He survived his bout with pneumonia but he almost didn't survive life with his mother. One night Tony was feeding the horses, making his way down the barn aisle with the food. He put Millie's feed in her tub, and then as he walked away, heard a squeal. O2B had gone over to the tub and stuck his nose in, and Millie, in another of her famous hissy fits, kicked. She got him right in the head, knocking him right back on his hocks. What next? Well, he did survive, but according to Tony, his head swelled horribly and he had a fracture right on the point of his cheekbone. I missed all this drama but he was weaned right after that, and the separation was mutually agreeable. Once again, the Ryans and Dr. Sue Montgomery gave him excellent care, and he got through that trauma well.

When a stall opened up at home, he came back to us. He spent lots of time in the stallion barn, in the nice roomy paddock, and showed the same quirks as his half-brother, picking up sticks and playing with horse toys. He was a humorous little guy but the more he matured, the more he looked like his father and seemed to have his disposition, too.

In my racing world, Suffolk Downs had closed, possibly forever and so we all migrated to Rockingham. In the barn where I had a stall for Reign, one of the other trainers, Mary Cameron, had a small farm nearby with a training track, so when it was time for O2B to be started under saddle, I thought it would be convenient to send him there, since it was so close to Rockingham, and then I could run over and watch his progress. Having survived pneumonia and then a facial fracture, our foal number eight was launched into the racing world!

Ebullient described him well. He was full of enthusiasm for everything: food, people, passing traffic, neighboring horses. He was cheerful, too and looked forward to going to the track. On his first trip there, he marched right out, started galloping, but when he got to the grandstand, he slowed up and just gawked at the grandstand, gawked at the other horses, gawked at the tote board, and completely ignored his rider so I turned to John Manning, the outrider, who was standing right next to me at the gap, and asked him to go retrieve him. He did and so the second day, we sent him out with a pony to babysit. He had been fine galloping on the Camerons' training track, but it was narrow, and just funneled him along. This one was like the wide-open spaces, and it was sensory overload for him.

It didn't take long for him to settle into the track routine, but you never knew when his good spirits would overwhelm him, or something would set him off into delirious leaping and plunging. This was not the kind of behavior exercise riders were fond of so I was fortunate to be able to call upon George Trenger again; he could sit through anything. O2B was a handsome colt, though, a miniature version of his gorgeous chestnut father, with a curvaceous, substantial body and "correct" legs.

His training proceeded at a normal rate through his two-year old summer. Then, we relocated to Suffolk for the fall, and he and Shine were installed in the same barn as my friend, Aimee Hall, and her husband, Jose Caraballo (Shine's jockey). Richard Trimmer was there, too so it was a congenial group. Little by little, Sunny Crime progressed. By late fall, he was breezing and doing gate work. This time, I had no trouble with Starter Tom. He got his gate card without incident. There was something about him, though, that was, well, goofy. Jim used to park by the barn on the way to work, and when he came back at night, he'd put their feed tubs in. One day, he came home and accosted me. "So! What has that horse done now?" "Huh?" "You probably didn't think I noticed, but he has some kind of trick shoe on." "Trick shoe?" "Yes! When I went to feed, he was standing at the door with some weird kind of metal cage on his foot, kind of like those salt-block holders."

I assured him that he had perfectly normal shoes, but I was apprehensive when I got to the barn in the morning. Sure enough, he was standing right at the door, waiting for the morning oats, and on his left foot, his metal salt-block holder! He must have been cavorting around in his stall, somehow knocked it right off the wall, and at some point stepped on it. It was jammed tight around his hoof. I had to get a hammer to knock it off. Richard Trimmer noted in his usual wry manner that this didn't bode well. A horse with lots of ability would have been crippled by doing that, and O2B seemed fine.

That was him! In January, the track publicity people came down to the barn to take a photo of one of Aimee's horses with a birthday cake. They were going to run a picture in the paper on January 1 of a horse celebrating the universal Thoroughbred birthday. Nice idea, but Aimee's horse was horrified at the sight of the cake and wouldn't come near it. They tried with every horse in her barn with no success. Then, they arrived at O2B's stall. He stuck his head out, sniffed the cake, and posed fetchingly with it.

Sunny Crime in the paddock with George.

Goofy or not, he finally was ready to run. That spring, Foxboro was opening. It was a small track with almost no barn area, but the management would van horses from Suffolk free of charge, and there was a maiden race scheduled that would suit him perfectly. I thought I'd support this program, so I entered him.

The van picked up a full load of horses, and O2B rode down without incident. He was always interested in anything new. This would be his debut. I don't think I would have done this with a normal horse, but he was just quirky enough to enjoy anything out of the routine. Years later, I remember little of that race. I know he didn't distinguish himself, but he didn't really have any problems. Then, when it was time to load up the van and return to Suffolk, we realized that there was no loading ramp. They had to drop the ramp right to the ground, making a steep incline. It was dark in the barn area, and lots of people leaving after the races were milling around. All the normal horses were leery of the setup and backing up when they were led over. Not O2B! He stepped out of the shadows, took one look at the near-vertical ramp, and marched right up.

After that uninspired beginning, he continued in the same vein. He ran three times after that, during the summer, at Rockingham. The best he could do was a weak fourth. Then, we moved back to Suffolk for the fall. Four starts there, and, again, nothing inspiring. He was handsome, and cheerful about his life at the racetrack, but with his blasé attitude toward competing, he was starting to remind me of Aggie.

Fall turned into winter. He ran three times. The first two were uninspiring, as usual, and his third start was downright brutal. It was a horrifically cold day: minus six! There were rumors about canceling all morning, but the first race went off on schedule. He was in the second, so when we got the call, we started up. I was walking with him, plodding with my head down to minimize the brutal force of the wind. My friend Mary Pitt was there, walking loyally beside me. As the horses from the first race passed us in their return to the stable area, we heard that my friend Jay Botty had won. That seemed like a good omen. I turned to Mary and said, "Well, he doesn't mind this frigid cold, I think if he's ever going to win a race, it will be today." I realized I had some money in my pocket, which was unusual for me, but I'd just cashed a check to buy groceries on the way home. I handed it to Mary, and told her to bet on him to win.

I never bet. I can actually recount every time I've done so. Most of the time, I'm just too busy when our own horses run and I'm superstitious. I don't want to jinx them. That day, however, it was just an impulse. That was the coldest day I can remember running a horse. The track was almost freeze-dried, and the jockeys all wore protective masks. Mary and I stood at my usual spot, next to the shrubs at the front of the paddock. The race went off without incident. I could see O2B running with the pack down the backside, then, as they turned for home, the whole field was foreshortened. I couldn't tell how he was placed but, little by little, as they came to the wire, he seemed to be churning along, closer and closer, and miracle of miracles he'd won.

Jim was wild. He ran over to us, exulting, and when I yanked on his sleeve and told him I'd bet forty to win, he was stunned. Naturally, given the horse's consistently dismal performance, the odds were long. He'd actually run the same as he'd always done, but he was oblivious to the crippling cold, just chugging along as the others fell back.

Sunny Crime (left) and his big sister Sunny Reign.

150

Jose rode up to us waving his whip, but he was so cold that he couldn't take off his gloves, or pull down his face mask so, in the win picture we have, he looks like the masked man. That wasn't our greatest victory, but it was one of the most memorable.

In the weeks to come, I did a reality check. He had run one more time, but he was distanced; it was even listed in the charts as a did-not-finish. He was as cheerful as ever, he looked great, but he had a tendon which was troublesome. I also reasoned that, even though he'd won a race, it might be another year before the stars aligned to have him win another. We had two more young horses coming along and I decided to retire him.

SUNNY CRIME: 11 starts / 1 win

```
                        SUNNY CRIME
OWNER                   SUFFOLK DOWNS           6.FURLONGS
SCHOOL HOUSE FARM                               JOSE C. CARABALLO
TRAINER                 2ND.PRINCE BERKLEY      TIME 1:19.2
SUSAN WALSH             3RD.BANJO JR.           FEB. 1,1993
```

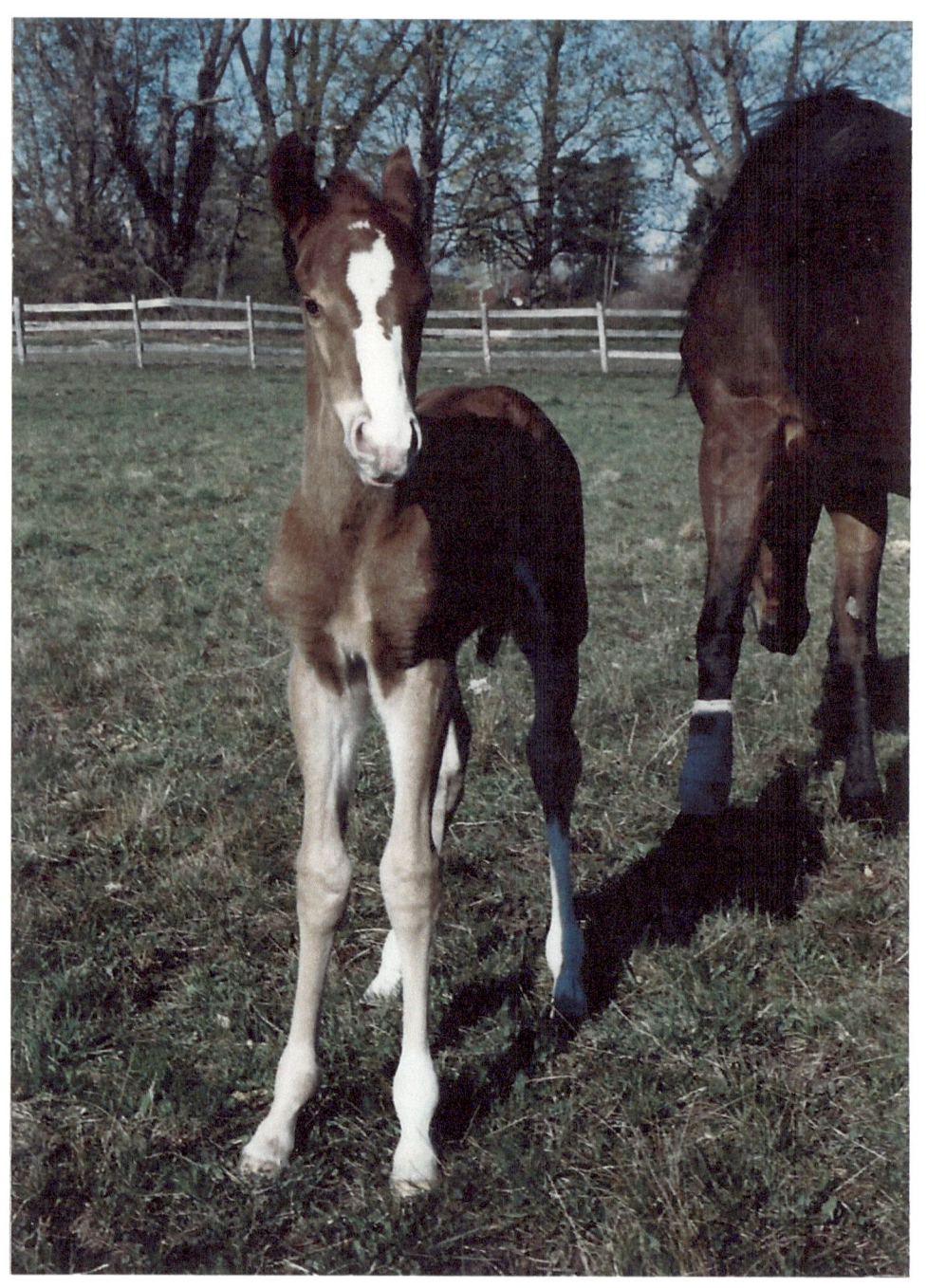

Sunny Stand (Macho)

After having my stallion, Sunny Clips, living offsite for three years, I suddenly had the chance to bring him home. The farm had acquired more and more boarders, but that winter a clump of them left, and Woody was having trouble replacing them. For the first time, they ran ads in the local horse papers, but there were still empty stalls, so he decided that I could bring Sunny home and keep him in the stud barn. Home he came. The day he arrived, all the boarders gathered to view my latest horse, and they were stunned into silence when he stepped off the van. He was a genuinely beautiful animal and the Ryans had him at a perfect weight, with a stunning metallic/copper coat.

Sunny loved his new home. He had a nice, roomy stall, and the adjacent paddock was not only roomy, but right along the road to the back field, so there was a constant stream of horses and riders walking by. Sunny was a quiet stallion. He'd walk up to the fence and watch the other horses go by, but rarely whinnied or ran the fence line. At some point, Woody realized that the back fence of that paddock was getting a little rickety, so he decreed that the only horse that could be turned out there was Sunny.

Sunny's stallion career was in its infancy. Sunny Reign was his first foal, and had yet to run; Sunny Crime was his second, but with the closing of Suffolk Downs, the breeding business in Massachusetts had cooled considerably. He did breed two outside mares, though; both large ponies, which was fine with him. Now, it was spring, and time to meet up once again with his number one girl, Lady. We had not bred her when Duly was a foal, but did breed her (many times) the following year with no luck. Now, once again, we brought them together. This time, Lady settled, and now, a year later, her due date approached.

Lady was now fifteen. She had always been fragile, but now, her locked ankle seemed even larger than before, and her rickety hind end seemed to give her more trouble than ever. Woody let us move her to the barn way in the back, the old bull barn. There was a good-sized stall there, and it opened up into a small paddock, so she could be outside even when she wasn't turned out in the field. I had figured that the more she moved around, the better. She had an uneventful pregnancy, but in the spring, when she was a good month from her due date, she started having real difficulty getting up. She and Duly were turned out together, which they loved, and they got lots of pasture time but sometimes I'd see her lying down, and I would have to run out and help when she wanted to get to her feet. Then, she started losing weight. Then, she started losing frightening amounts of weight. She got to the point where she was so thin that I thought she couldn't possibly be in foal. Looking at her emaciated body, I couldn't see where a foal could be hiding.

We were concerned, so we summoned the vet. Dr. Orcutt, the son, showed up and gave her a careful exam. He put on his plastic sleeve and felt inside. In typical dry humor, he looked over at me and said quietly, "Well, there is definitely a large foot in here."

We had planned to let her foal in the root cellar, where she'd had Reign, so we cleaned it up and filled it with fresh straw and let her settle in. During the day, she still went out with Duly, but at night, she was down there, and I started nightly checks. The vet had stressed that it was important for me to be there when she foaled, since she seemed so decrepit and thin, but once again, this was not her first foal, and like most mares, she preferred to be alone. I spent four nights checking constantly, with no success. Each time, I'd sneak into the tack room upstairs and quietly walk down the stairs and peer in. Each time, she'd look over from eating her hay and give me an annoyed look, but no foal.

Meanwhile, my other lives went on: the racetrack early in the morning, then school, then back to the farm. On the fourth day of fruitless vigils, I whined to my vet, Marty Simensen, saying I was so tired that I'd probably sleep through the whole thing.

Marty paused, then said, "Foal alert!" His wife had a "foal alert" device which she wasn't using at the time. I could borrow that, and it would let me know when her contractions began. Then I could get a good night's sleep.

Perfect! On the way home from school that day, I made a detour to Hamilton and picked up the high-tech device from his wife. That afternoon, I rigged it up. It consisted of a surcingle, with a yoke that went around her neck. The yoke had a sensor on the inside, which would set off an alarm when it became moist. The theory was when she started labor and sweated, the sensor would alert us and we'd have time to run over. The alarm was a separate unit that plugged in at our house, with an antenna. Great! I set up the alarm in the bedroom window and pointed it right at the barn, then went to Lady and put on the surcingle and yoke. Jim was at home, resting, skeptical at this modern invention. I got everything in place, then wetted a finger and touched the sensor. Back at the house, the alarm went off right by Jim's head. He and the dog were not amused.

I knew it worked and that night I went to bed and had a wonderful full night's sleep. The next night, I settled Lady in, and went to sleep again, content in the fact that the contraption would let me know in plenty of time to be over there.

Just after midnight, the alarm sounded. I snapped awake, leapt out of bed, jumped into my waiting jeans and boots, and ran to the barn. I was there in no more than two minutes. I slipped into the main floor; everything was quiet. I went into the tack room and tiptoed down the stairs. Not a sound! I could look through the little windows and see Lady over by her hay, grazing, and alone. Huh, I thought, well, maybe Jim was right to be skeptical. Then, I quietly pushed open the door at the bottom of the stairs.

Hello! A big, handsome colt looked right back at me. He was standing right there, alert, all dry, bright-eyed and, yes, bushy-tailed and probably at least an hour old. He was right in my face, too; he pushed his nose right into my hand to say hello. Then, he turned around and marched over to Lady and bullied his way up into her udder for a drink.

When I got a look at Lady and felt her dry, unruffled coat, I theorized that her labor had been so easy that she'd never broken a sweat, but at some point, the foal had chewed on the yoke where the sensor was and triggered the alarm. So much for high technology!

It was a relief to have Lady foal so easily and this foal was obviously healthy, too. He was bright chestnut, like his father, with flashy white legs, and a white blaze but his blaze was atypical. If viewed sideways, the top part looked like the map of Massachusetts. It gave him a rakish, unconventional look that fitted perfectly with his look-at-me attitude.

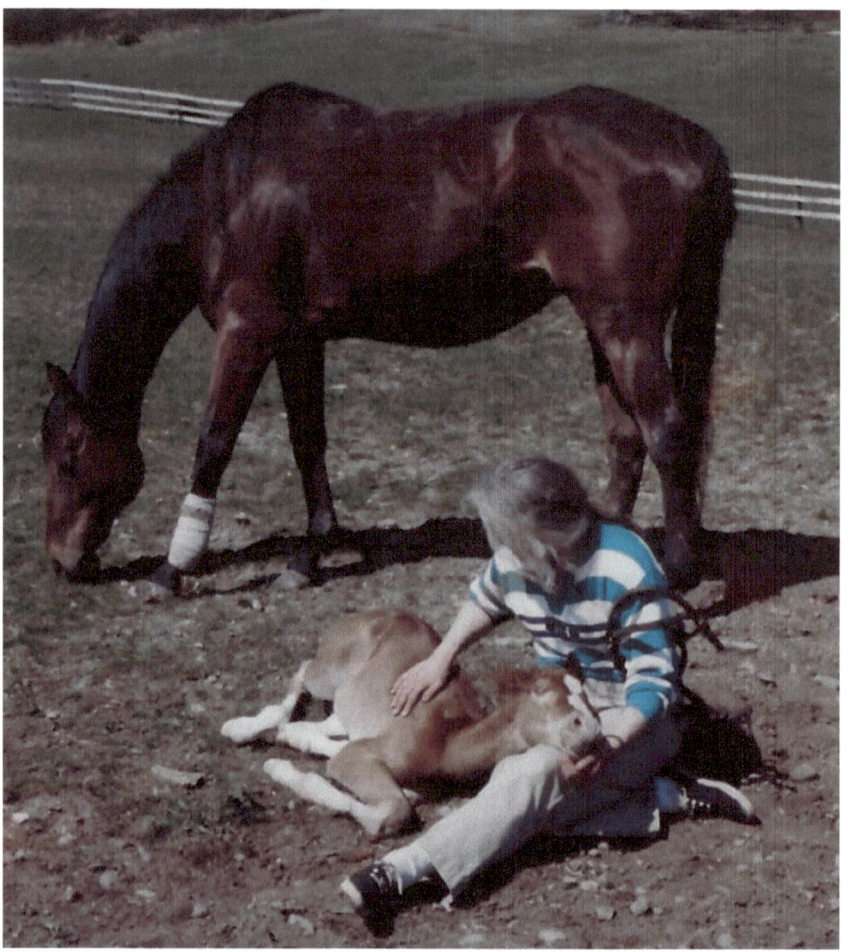

Royal Stand (Lady) and an eight hour old Sunny Stand.

The next day, we turned them out in the pasture. For a day-old foal, this was no small feat. They had to walk out through the side barnyard, up the drive around to the front of the barn, through the large riding ring, and finally to their pasture. Since this was not her first foal, Lady was good about it, peacefully strolling alongside Jim. I walked behind, both arms around the foal's body, encouraging him to move forward. By the time we'd made it to the pasture, both he and I were exhausted. One of the first pictures we have of him is me sitting down in the dirt and him flopped into my lap.

Sunny Stand with Royal Stand meets my oldest sister, Jeanne.
Jeanne took me to the races when I was 15.

Now for the name. Sunny Clips/ Royal Stand had already given us Sunny Reign. Now, the Jockey Club approved his name, Sunny Stand. From day one, however, looking at his in-your-face attitude, everyone called him Macho.

Macho's first seven weeks passed uneventfully. The weather was idyllic, so he got plenty of pasture time, and there were always horses turned out in the pasture next to his, and people riding in the ring on the other side of his gate, so there was plenty to see. Lady was gaining weight, too. Without his enormous body pressing on her innards, she was much sounder, and the spring grass agreed with her, too.

Macho! That was the nickname that followed him through life. It was appropriate when he was a little foal with a big ego, and it continued to be fitting when he was at the track racing as well. When he arrived at Rockingham from Norman Hall's as a two year old, all fit and broke, he was bursting with good spirits. He was already muscled out, he had a robust body, and was quite full of himself. For the first day or so, I was lucky to get the same rider he'd had at Hall's, so he started off well but his high spirits intimidated people. I went through riders at an amazing rate. They'd be willing enough at first, but when he dragged them to the track, semi-reared and did pirouettes crossing the street, they tended to be all booked for the next day. One rider said to me as he mounted up and walked down the shedrow, "You had the rest now you got the best." He disappeared around the corner, I turned around and started back to meet up with him outside, then heard a commotion.

They'd been walking down the backside of the barn when Macho turned and started ducking out of the shed, caught his toe on the edging, and fell right out of the barn in a heap. He was fine, and the rider had bailed out, unhurt and they continued on to the track, but the next day the rider told me, sorry, he was all booked up!

One day, I was coming back from the track with Macho and yet another exercise rider. Just as we got to the gap, he started acting up, feeling good, and Aimee Hall was riding to the track on her horse. She was horrified; she didn't want people thinking that a graduate of Norman Hall's track would be that fractious; so the next day, she showed up at the barn, had me give her a leg up, and went off and galloped him herself. Finally, after going through a series of riders, each bigger and stronger than the next, I tried a different tack: a girl. It turns out that the one who galloped him best was Maureen Blanchette, a diminutive exercise girl who later rode races. She would just sweet-talk him to the track, humor him around, and give him lots of praise and attention on the way back. He loved her.

By the end of the summer, Macho was galloping properly, had worked a few times, and was making progress. We moved back to Suffolk in the fall, and his training continued. At Suffolk, I found another female exercise rider, Dorothy Gertner, and she was just short of fabulous. She'd been an exercise rider in New York, and treated him like one of Shug McGaughey's: walking to the track slowly, galloping strongly, then pulling up and standing, and meandering back to the barn, stopping to graze at whatever tufts of grass he could find. He loved Dorothy and he was fast approaching being race-ready.

The final hurdle: the starting gate! He was, of course, a full brother to Sunny Reign, who'd been my action-packed introduction to our starter, Tom Schwigen. He'd been exposed to handling by many more people than she, though and I thought he'd be fine. Now the quest for the gate card began. He'd been over there for preliminaries without incident, so I thought he'd be good but we were fast approaching his first race, and it was time to get the official card, so once again, I borrowed a bike and pedaled over to the gate one morning.

As I drew up, Tom yelled, "Here comes Auntie Em!" and when I explained I wanted to get Macho's gate card, he was amenable. Macho approached, Jose riding, and Aimee Hall leading him on her pony, Bandit, an ex-racehorse. They milled around behind the gate, waited for a few others to load and go; then walked in. The starters shut the doors, and he stood a bit nervously, and then they opened the gate and he roared out. He breezed a good half mile, and I was thrilled but Tom was less than impressed. He felt he was too antsy in the gate, and hadn't left there fast enough. He also hadn't broken "with the bell," a requirement for his gate card. The next day, I pled my case to the starter. I told him I needed to enter Macho in two days, if he were to run that weekend, so he suggested I bring him back. If he broke sharply, with the bell, he'd give him his card.

Wednesday! That was only two days after his half-mile breeze, but we all headed to the gate: me on a bike, Jose on Macho, Aimee on her pony, Bandit. We got there a little past nine, ready to breeze. We stood around behind the gate for a while, and then Tom looked at me and smiled.

"Well, little lady, looks like you're out of luck! He'll get his card when he breezes from the gate, with the bell, *with company*. Now, it's almost nine-thirty, and there isn't no one else in sight!"

I was devastated. I had to enter him that morning. The race Saturday was perfect for him, he was fit and ready. Now, before I could even express my dismay, Aimee turned in the saddle and yelled over, "Take the rings off this horse! I want a six-month card for Bandit Boy!"

A starter walked over and removed the rings from her horse, Bandit, who was, in fact, a former race horse, and she rode him into a stall. Macho walked into the one beside her, the starters slammed the doors behind them, Tom hit the button, the bell rang and they were off! I heard Jose yell, "Hold back, Aimee!" in the first few strides, and then Macho kicked into gear, and his big red hind end disappeared into the distance. By the time I met him back at the barn, cooled him out, and went back to the secretary's office, Tom had filed his gate card, so I entered him in his first race, which happened to be, appropriately enough, The Norman Hall Stakes, a race for two year olds named in honor of Aimee's grandfather.

Sunny Stand with Robbie Holman in the Suffolk Downs paddock.

Saturday arrived. Robbie Holman led Macho to the paddock, and I walked along with him. Aimee was there already, prepared to present the trophy. Her brother Joe was there, too, and her aunt Holly. Two of my friends from home, Carrie Weeks and Denise Dunn, had come to see him make his debut. They both had horses at the farm, and they'd been there when he was born. Macho did a little gawking when he came into the paddock and saw the crowd, but he strutted around confidently. He stood well as I saddled him, and soon he and Jose were on the track warming up. It was a sprint, so the gate was way across the infield. I took up my usual spot, in the bushes at the edge of the paddock, and suddenly they were off. Within a few strides, he was at the head of the pack. The field made the turn and straightened out for the stretch drive, and I could see that big white blaze out in front. I heard Larry Collmus announcing, "Sunny Stand is in front-and he is a runner!" He'd won!

We went wild! Jim was yelling, I was yelling and as Jose rode him back to the winner's circle, Carrie and Denise appeared. Denise said to me, "I'd never understood why you'd spend so much time at the track, every day, all those years-but now?" She was speechless!

Macho stood for his win picture like a pro. Jose jumped off, the valet unsaddled him, and Robbie and I headed back to the test barn. As I walked back, lugging the huge trophy, Aimee Hall came running over. We were hugging and jumping and grinning, behaving like idiots; and suddenly Tom Schwigen was there. "Well, girls, guess he can run a little!" he said, and gave us a hug, too.

If this were fiction, a rainbow would appear, and he'd go on to fame and fortune, but alas, this is real life. A few days after the race, I had the vets x-ray his knees, and confirmed what I'd suspected: chips. I had always worried about his soundness. Like his half-sister, Duly, he had odd feet. His heels were very low, and he had a strange angle to the front of his hoofs; they almost looked like duck feet. I'd tried all kinds of shoes and pads, but the hoofs were just odd. He'd tend to get sore-footed, too, and sometimes had a stabbing way of walking, scuffling like an old man trying to keep his slippers on. This went way back. I remember walking him to the pasture when he was a yearling and thinking he was stabbing. Was this the chicken or the egg? Did his weird feet and the stabbing way of going cause his knees? Whatever the cause, the result was chips, so after his big victory, he was on his way to Tufts for surgery.

After the surgery, he went back to the track. It was easier dealing with him there than at home. I could walk him in the shedrow no matter what the weather, and he was content enough there. At home, he'd want to get turned out and that was not an option. He recovered well, and in the spring ran in another Massbred stakes, "The African Prince," and won again. Then, off to Rockingham for the summer. There, he ran in a race for horses who hadn't won three races. He got into a speed duel and tired; but when I ran him back in the next race, he rated nicely, having learned from that experience; and he won again. In the fall, back to Suffolk. He ran opening day of the fall meet in the Great Mystery stakes and yes, won it! This was gratifying: I had had a share in Great Mystery when he was at stud, and had two foals from that: Aggie and the Rodent, neither of whom accomplished anything at the track. Macho had now won four of his first five starts.

A few weeks after that race, we had another win: the New England Turf Writers had voted him the best three-year old. Not the best Massbred three-year-old, but the best of all! It was a stunning accolade for us. The horse we'd bred ourselves, practically in our front yard, and delivered and raised at home, had been voted over royally bred horses from Kentucky, Florida, and elsewhere. Amazing!

Once again, however, having race horses was very much good news/bad news. The good news, of course, was a horse who'd won four of his first five races, and been voted Best New England Three-year Old. The bad news: his glass knees/feet were going to compromise his career. Jose Caraballo, his loyal jockey, had said to me once after a work that if he didn't have those problems, he could have won in New York. We tried to cope. Mr. Kirby, who was the patriarch of our barn, offered us the use of his whirlpool boots. Yes, whirlpool boots. These used to be a part of every barn, but were hard to find now. They were giant rubber boots, like fireman's boots, but with hoof-shaped feet; and they attached to a pump, which, when plugged in, agitated the water: a whirlpool for legs.

Macho stepped into them grudgingly the first time, but when I filled them with hot water and plugged them in, and he felt the bubbling heat around his knees and feet, he relaxed immediately. He would stand motionless for a full hour while the water and the bubbles worked their magic; so this became our treatment of choice. Every day. Every day, including Thanksgiving and Christmas. On dark days, once training was over and everyone's horses had been fed, I'd often be the only one in the barn, sitting outside his stall, reading, while the boots churned and roiled.

Sunny Stand with Jose Caraballo.

He ran one more time at three, in a Massbred stakes late in the year. It was a distance race, but I didn't think that would be a problem. He ran well for most of the race, but in the stretch, he seemed to tire, and just missed, finishing second. We were disappointed, and I blamed myself for running him when he was possibly not fit but as he cooled out, we realized fitness wasn't the issue: he bled. Something was not right; once again, his knees and feet were his Achilles heel.

That winter, as he was turning four, he had surgery again. Again, he recuperated at the track, with daily whirlpool sessions and range-of-motion exercises. His exercise rider, Dorothy, relocated to New York, but she recommended a replacement: Greg Knight. Greg was from California, from a family of horsemen, which was obvious from the first time I gave him a leg up. He suited Macho perfectly. Their gallops were beautiful to watch, and his input was invaluable. We soldiered on.

As a four year old, Macho only ran twice. I gave him a long time to get over his second surgery. He went to Rockingham for the summer with the other horses, but he didn't run until late fall when he was back in Boston. The results were disappointing. Fall turned to winter, and suddenly he was five. He enjoyed being at the track; he loved all the attention he got from everyone, and looked forward to galloping. That spring, he ran two more times, but, again, the results were disappointing. Greg had trimmed down to where he was riding weight, and had started riding races in the afternoon, so Macho ran one more time with his buddy Greg in the irons. Once again, if this were fiction, it would have made a nice ending, but in real life, he just couldn't ratchet himself up from galloping to racing. The race was a letdown to us all. I had to face the fact that his glass knees and feet were limiting what he could do in the afternoon. Reluctantly, knowing how much he enjoyed being at the track, we retired him and took him home.

Sunny Stand: 11 starts / 4 wins (3 stakes) / 1 second

THE AFRICAN PRINCE STAKES
$25,000 ADDED

Sunny Stand

SUFFOLK DOWNS

School House Farm's
Susan Walsh, Trainer
Jose Caraballo, Rider
6 Furlongs 1:11

Potential Fire 2nd
Atta Speed 3rd
April 23, 1994
© Equi–Photo

SCHOOL HOUSE FARM OWNER
SUSAN WALSH TRAINER
JOSE C. CARABALLO UP
PURSE $12,000

SUNNY STAND

ROCKINGHAM PARK

BARNEY GOO GOO 2ND
LOVESHACH 3RD
6 FURLONGS 1:12
OCTOBER 5, 1994
© 1994 HODGES PHOTOGRAPHY

THE GREAT MYSTERY STAKES
$25,000 Added

Sunny Stand

SUFFOLK DOWNS

School House Farm's
Susan Walsh, Trainer
Jose Caraballo, Rider
6 Furlongs 1:14 1/5

Fleet Rise 2nd
Potential Dreamer 3rd
October 21, 1994
© Equi-Photo

"Though she be but little, she is fierce." — William Shakespeare

Due To Land (Teeny)

We had retired Duly the previous year from a long, successful career at the track. She was at Rockingham after Suffolk had closed, and when we decided to retire her, we sent her right from the track to Maryland. Once again, we wanted two foals. We were breeding Lady to Sunny that spring, but Duly had been such a good horse at the track that we thought it would be smart to breed her to a stallion who had some statistics behind him, so off she went. Cooper, the C&W van driver, picked her up at the track, and when I brought her out, he whistled at the sight of her. She was gleaming and dappled like a wet seal, and much more voluptuous than the usual fit race horse. He smiled and said that she'd be the best-looking broodmare on the farm.

Duly was seven years old. I had foaled her out myself, and, except for the two weeks she'd spent at Norman Hall's farm being broke, she'd always been with us. This time, she was only gone for less than two months, but we missed her terribly. Finally, we got the news from Maryland: she was indeed in foal to Assault Landing, and we could bring her home.

The night she was due to arrive, I parked the truck next to the barn to wait. Naturally, there were delays: Maryland-to-Massachusetts was a long haul, with lots of opportunity for traffic problems. She was late, then even later, and I ended up spending the night sitting in my truck at the barn. Finally, early the next morning, I heard the sound of a big rig. There she was! I got out of the truck and stood in the road watching as Cooper drove the big van up the road to the barn. Cooper was leaning out his window, and I could see, in the back, Duly's nose, sticking out her window. I called her name, smiling, and then Cooper yelled out, "You won't be smiling when you see the rest of her!"

He was right. When she walked off the van, I was horrified: her beautiful shiny black coat was now a dull sun-burned peanut-butter, and she was covered in marks that looked suspiciously like scabs from kicks. She was also very thin and footsore. Jim came walking up then, and was stunned, then angry, and stormed off to get to the phone.

Well, when we talked to the farm, we got a profuse apology and an explanation. They turned the mares out all together, and she got "initiated" by some of the others. They also kept them out all day, and the Maryland sun was merciless to her hothouse coat. Yes, it was hard to see how bad she looked, BUT, she was in foal, and that was the point.

It didn't take long for her to recover from her Maryland adventure. Being turned out all day with her mother, Lady, did wonders for her mental attitude and the nice spring grass was the best tonic she could ask for. She and Lady settled down to a nice routine of companionable grazing all through their pregnancies. Lady was the first to foal. Once she had produced Macho, she and he took over that pasture, so we moved Duly to the stud barn to await the birth of her foal.

Once again, it was easy to get my timing right with first foals, since the mare didn't know what was about to change her life, so she didn't get cagey and secretive. Five weeks after Lady foaled, Duly's udder filled to capacity, and then one afternoon, waxed up. Once again, I hovered around all evening. The stud barn was nice and quiet. All the boarders were over at the main barn, and again, I could sneak in through the back door. The third time that night that I slipped in, I heard the usual rustling from all the other stalls, and from hers, soft groans. She had just gone down, and as I watched, a powerful contraction gripped her abdomen. Jim had bemoaned the fact that he'd never seen a birth, and I knew he was still up, so I ran back to our house to alert him, and in minutes, he was there, watching nervously from the aisle. Duly didn't mind my presence in the stall; she was focused on her own body. She was made to be a broodmare. In minutes, with almost minimal help from me, a tiny foal emerged. I pulled the caul back over her head, and she shook her ears, then dove the rest of the way into the waiting straw. Again, the little bleat. Again, the mare's stunned reaction, and again, the answering call. The foal started moving her little legs right away, and very quickly managed to struggle to her feet. Duly instinctively hovered over her, licking her protectively. A tiny filly, but lively. Jim, observing his first foaling, was stunned at first but then, as the foal tottered around, said, "That's it?"

Compared to the commanding presence of Macho as a foal, she was, well, tiny. She was a little mulish, too: a bland gray/brown, with short little legs. The product of the biggest stud fee we'd ever paid and our winningest, most curvaceous mare was this funny little burro. Jim said, "That's the homeliest foal I've ever seen."

Duly, though, was impressed. She couldn't stop licking and nudging, and kept up a constant low nickering. We had a few wonderful minutes, standing there in the quiet, watching Duly help her firstborn begin her life. I went back outside the stall, and we just savored those first moments. Then, the foal walked around Duly, and when she turned to follow, her hind end swung into view. Jim was horrified. "She's prolapsing her uterus! She's having another one!"

We stared: an enormous round mass was bulging out beneath her tail. She showed signs of discomfort, too. I slipped into the stall again to get a better look. It was a grapefruit-sized mass, quite hard, but cold to the touch. We didn't hesitate. I ran back to the house and called the vet.

The next hour or so, we hovered around. Duly seemed uncomfortable, but never stopped ministering to her baby. The baby was fine, gaining coordination by the minute, quick to nurse and lively.

Finally, after what seemed an eternity, we heard the sound of the vet's car, and in she came. This time, it was Helen, Dr. Orcutt's daughter. She was an excellent vet in her own right, and had done post-graduate work with mares and foals. She was calm and focused. She went right to the stall and examined Duly, and then reassured us. It was not a uterus we were staring at, but a haematoma. Straining in labor, Duly had somehow overdone it. Helen gave her a little medication for her discomfort, and said she'd return in the morning to check her again. Another curious development: for the first and last time foaling out our mares, I found what my friend Mrs. Dudley called the rubber ducky, or in horsemen's books, the hippomane. This was a little spongy piece of matter that was in the birth sack, and which some thought was held in the foal's mouth when in the uterus to keep fluid out of his lungs. An odd little artifact.

By morning, all of us were in better shape. The foal was wild now, bucking and squealing like a little piglet, racing through the straw. Duly was much more comfortable, and the ugly hematoma seemed much reduced in size. Everything looked better in the light of dawn.

The weather was in our favor, too. It was a nice, mild day, so we turned Duly and the foal out in the small paddock right across from their stall. As we stood at the door admiring them, Dr. Orcutt appeared. Helen was on another call, so he came by to check. Jim once again said that the foal was pretty ugly, I said she looked like a tarantula, and Dr. Orcutt commented that maybe she was a wildebeest. Whatever she looked like, Duly thought she was priceless, and the foal herself was unperturbed. She was constantly in motion, racing around the paddock, spinning, stopping, skipping over the ground. As a racehorse-to-be, that was more important than what she looked like, anyway. Duly herself, who had matured into a stunning mare, had been a little odd looking in her first days. We were just thrilled that the labor was over, and the foal was so healthy.

Jim worked on her official name, Assault Landing/Duly Royal. Well, she was so small that we were already calling her Teeny. He came up with Assaulted Peanut as his first choice, which we thought was hilarious. The Jockey Club, however, was not amused, so we made a second choice, which they accepted: Due to Land. Every day, though, for us, it was Teeny.

We left the two of them in the stud barn for the first two weeks. They could spend the whole day out in the paddock, and they seemed fine. I was avoiding the next step: turning them out with Lady and Macho. Macho was five weeks older than Duly's foal, and in those five weeks he had become even more confident and powerful. What would he do to this little tarantula when he saw her?

After two weeks, though, it was time. Duly was getting bored in the small paddock, and they had grazed it down to dirt, so we held our breaths and set out. We turned Lady and Macho out, then came back for Duly. We took her out the side door. Jim led her and I followed behind, scooping up Teeny and keeping her walking right behind her mother. We made our way across the yard, then into the ring and headed to the pasture gate. By the time we were halfway across the ring, Macho had spotted us. Lady saw Duly, and slowly made her way down the hill to greet her. Macho tore down the hill and stood right at the gate, staring. Somehow, we managed to get Duly and the foal into the field, and stepped back. Macho raced over to the foal, towering over her, head raised. Teeny? She took one look at this monster, spun around, and hit him in the chest with both her baby hind legs. Macho stepped back in shock, and she spun around with her teeth bared. He lowered his head, they sniffed and from that moment on, were fast friends.

Once again, as with Duly and Aggie, having two foals made things much easier. The two mares grazed all day, side by side, and Teeny and Macho ripped around constantly. As big as he was, she was much sharper; he always deferred to her, which was fun to watch. Spring flowed into summer, and then fall, and the two of them grew stronger. When it was time to wean, we waited until Teeny was six months old, and tried a new method. One day, we brought them all in, and then subtracted Lady. The next day, we turned Duly and Teeny out, and then Macho, and he went right over to Teeny as he usually did, his mother just a memory. It was the easiest weaning to date. Then, a few days later, we repeated the procedure with Teeny and Duly. The next morning, Macho and Teeny went out together, with no mares. Simple! There was an embarrassing moment when Teeny wanted to nurse, realized there was no convenient mare nearby with a full udder, and tried to nurse on Macho's well, appendage…but she realized quickly that it was pointless.

Teeny and Macho had a great childhood. They made it through the winter with no problems, went through their yearling year without a hitch, and were always getting attention from anyone in the area. One day, I was heading out to bring them in. It was hot and humid, so Macho was standing right at the gate waiting, and when I was halfway across the ring, he suddenly reared up and jumped right over the gate and landed awkwardly in the ring. I have no idea what made him do that, but I caught him without a problem, and Teeny was right there, too. He had a few dings on his front legs, but was fine. That didn't bode well for a possible career as a hunter/jumper, but he wasn't fazed by that incident at all.

One day, we woke up and realized that they were both two year olds. Two! I was so busy dealing with the horses at the track that I hadn't had time to begin breaking them. I went through my "lead-to-pasture-with-tack" method, and they accepted all that very quickly. We decided to send them both to Norman Hall's to train before going to the track, and Macho, being older, went first. Once again, I called my friend Joe Moore, and one day he arrived with his nice, big trailer. He set up a box stall, and parked in front of the barn with the side ramp dropped. Macho walked out confidently, stared boldly at the ramp, and after pausing for a minute, marched right on.

Sunny Stand and his best friend, Due to Land, with her mother Duly Royal.

When Macho had gone, I spent more time with Teeny. She was used to being tacked, but I found time to get her into the round pen and start long lines with her. She was still "teeny," of course; but she had a stubborn, feisty streak in her, so the boarders were expecting some real action. She was feisty, yes, but she was also very smart and naturally curious, and she turned out to be a star pupil. She loved the long-lining, and really enjoyed taking trips all around the farm. One of my favorite pictures is one of her on the back road in all the gear, with me standing behind her.

Macho's training at the Halls went well, and it wasn't long before they thought he was ready for the track, so off he went. Then, Teeny took his place. When Joe came for her, I wanted to go along, so I rode right in the back. It was an interesting trip. She'd never been trailered, never even practiced (since my old trailer was gone), so she was nervous for the first mile, but then she found a way to stand in the box stall that was comfortable for her, and she rode the rest of the way quietly. It was a long trip, and when we were on the highway with big trucks going by, the noise was pulled right into her stall but she was unruffled. I was more stressed out than she was.

Once the staff at the Halls was satisfied with her progress, she joined Macho at the track. Foals nine and ten were on their way.

All the time Macho was at the track, his childhood friend, Teeny, was stabled in the stall right next to him. She was a complete contrast to him. Where he was tall and robust, with a blinding chestnut coat and lots of "chrome," she was tiny, with short little legs, and a drab dark brown, with no markings at all. He attracted attention with his flamboyant looks, and she was always under the radar, but I knew that all the time they were growing up, galloping around the pasture, she was his equal and, most of the time, called the shots.

She may have been teeny, but she was also feisty. Fortunately for all involved, she loved going to the track and galloping and she got along splendidly with Maureen Blanchette, her exercise rider. Maureen was tactful enough to handle Macho, and she soon realized that the best way to get along with Teeny was to be as unobtrusive as possible, so when they settled in at Suffolk Downs for the fall meet, things went well.

We had never had horses ready to run as two year olds except for Duly, who first ran in December of her second year. Due to one thing or another, all our previous horses had hit some minor snag, or were slow in their training, so that they didn't make their debuts until three. Now, though, these two were getting fit, and fast, so much to my surprise, I realized that both of them might be ready to run before the year's end.

Teeny was very competitive. Once, I wanted to breeze her a half mile in company, so I asked around and found my friend Dennis Wallace had a colt looking to do the same. We agreed to go together, so that morning he came by the barn on the way to the track, and we walked over together. As we followed the two horses, I had to laugh. Dennis' colt was an enormous, gangly horse, and Teeny, marching along next to him, looked like his foal. Dennis even made a comment about having the two stay together at first, but when they came out of the turn for home, I shouldn't feel bad if his horse drew off. "Let's face it: his stride has to be twice as long as hers." We stood at the quarter pole and watched them gallop off together. They came down the backside and started to breeze right on cue, came by us together although Teeny's feet were moving at twice the rate of his, and then, when they turned for home, she pinned her ears and left him in the lurch! A sweet moment.

The last stumbling block to making her debut was, of course, getting her gate card. Thinking of the battle I'd gone through with Shine, and then Macho, I dreaded sending Teeny over to the gate in the morning. She was willful and opinionated. If she didn't like doing something, it didn't get done without a battle. Still, there was no way around this, so I borrowed a bike once again and peddled over.

I stood next to Starter Tom that morning and explained who was on her way over. I must have had a look of complete horror on my face because Tom patted my shoulder and smiled at me as Teeny trotted around behind the gate and came to a stop. I held my breath; a starter walked toward her, but Maureen waved him back. They opened the back gates, she walked in on her own and stood, they shut the gates behind her, and then opened them in front of her. She galloped out. Tom looked at me and smiled: "You can relax. This little filly is smart; she's gonna be fine." She was! In two more trips, she had the coveted gate card and was ready to run.

Now, it was December. The race she was aiming for was the Massachusetts Futurity, for two-year-old Massbreds. Macho had won his debut two weeks before. Several horses from that race were running back in this one, but he was headed for surgery. Teeny would have to be our hope in this one.

Teeny in the paddock at Suffolk Downs with
Robby Holman, a superior horseman!

Once again, Robby Holman was my main man, taking Teeny to the paddock while I walked along with them. Teeny got along fine with me, and tolerated Maureen, but had an innate dislike for all other humans, yet Robby's professional, firm approach seemed to work. I don't remember much about the walk over, the paddock, or the post parade. The chart of the race mentions that she was "fractious in the paddock," which was an unusual comment: she must have been wild. Still, she made it through the post parade, walked into the gate on her own, and they were off. As they went down the backstretch, she was in mid-pack, but as they headed into the turn, she started passing horses. I could see her moving fast on the outside and as they all headed down the stretch, I thought, "Could we really have two horses and two winning debuts?"

Well, just as I thought that was to be, she slowed dramatically. I blamed myself. I knew she was competitive but she must have tired. Her not being fit enough was my fault. When they came back, the jockey said simply, "She stopped." Robbie and I took her back to the barn. I'd already set up bath water, so Robbie held her outside the barn while I washed her off. I thought to myself that she was oddly quiet. Usually, she shuffled around while I was bathing her. Then, when I'd finished and Robbie went to lead her away, she stood frozen to the spot. She could not move, not wouldn't move-couldn't move! A few times recently, she'd done this coming back from training: stopping in the shedrow and not wanting to move. At first, we thought she was tying up, but after a few minutes, she seemed fine, so we shrugged it off. Now, though, she was locked in place.

We called the vet, of course, who gave her some medication for pain, and suggested x-rays of her stifle. There was no way we could walk her out. We just let her stand outside until she dried, and then ever so slowly and gingerly, returned her to her stall. I stood in her stall with her, feeling the letdown. It was so odd to see her not moving around. Just when I thought I couldn't feel any worse, I heard a voice through the back wall: a trainer who had horses on the other side of the barn. "I feel bad for that girl. She ran that filly of hers today, her first race, and she's done!"

The next morning, she seemed, if not back to normal, at least improved. She could walk around her stall, and was eager to eat. We left her in, and the vet came over to x-ray her stifle, right in her stall. The next day, she was more herself, and then late in the morning our vet came over holding the x-rays, with a funny look on her face. "The stifle x-rays look fine," she said. "BUT, I was going over them with Mary Kahn, and she noticed this: way down at the bottom of the x-ray, you can see the tibia and right there (pointing) is a stress fracture!"

Well, that explained the times she'd stopped after galloping, when we thought she was tying up. There was a good side to this: it was an injury that wouldn't need any surgery or expensive treatment, just rest and limited activity. As winter set in, both Macho and Teeny were on R&R. Teeny had stall rest for a while, and then twice-daily walks around the shedrow, which we could do every day, rain, shine, or, in this case, snow. Finally, when x-rays showed the fracture had healed, she went back to long jogs on the track, and then galloping. With her vivacious personality, she never really lost fitness, and when she went back to galloping, she did it with such aggressiveness that I was afraid it would aggravate her problems, so I did something I never had done, and never did again: I sent her to the track ponying, without a rider. I reasoned that at least she wouldn't be carrying weight, so Cathy Chumbley agreed to take her on.

Cathy picked her up at the barn. She always had wonderful ponies who were used to anything, and this one stoically marched to the track with Teeny in tow. They set off at a good pace, and I watched them make a circuit of the track, then pull up and walk off. I thought this would work, but Chumbley had a request. "You've got to put blinkers on her! She's doing fine with the pony, but when she looks up and sees me, she tries to hit the brakes!" She was right; Teeny was not a "people person," so from then on, she went out with blinkers.

Teeny was quick to get back in shape. She ran three times at Suffolk that spring. The second time she ran, Rudy Baez rode her. He was a perennial leading rider and we were fortunate to get him. He rode her brilliantly. She came in second, even though she was blocked coming out of the turn. When we ran her back after that, Rudy was on another mount, so my friend Mary Pitt suggested Bill Klinke. Of course! He'd ridden her mother, Duly, with great results. He agreed, and rode her to victory.

That was a particularly satisfying win. I couldn't help thinking back to that dark day in winter when she came back from her debut and froze up, and I heard another trainer say she was "all done." She relished racing, too, and even though the jockey had to be careful getting off, doing a flying leap to avoid her lethal heels, everyone agreed that she was very competitive.

Soon after that victory, Suffolk closed for the summer, and we moved to Rockingham. I was assigned stalls in the barn that was right alongside the turn and Teeny and Macho had stalls looking right onto the track. I thought this would be a problem, but, on the contrary, it was a blessing. It gave them something to do in the afternoon. As soon as the sound of the gate opening went over the intercom, all the horses on that side of the barn came to the front of their stalls, stood and watched until the field roared by, and then went back to what they'd been doing.

The day we moved in, I settled them into their new stalls. I had stall screens in their doors, rather than webbings. I didn't want Macho crashing through, and I didn't want to tempt Teeny into sneaking under. I spent that day settling them in, moving all my gear into a tack room, and making sure they were alright. I could park right near the barn, too, in sight of the stalls. I realized only too late that this was a bad idea. When I'd decided that they'd be good until night feed time, I went to the truck and drove off, planning to go home until later. I'd just started down the back road when I heard a crash. I looked in the rear-view mirror to see Teeny running after me! I stopped, caught her, returned her to the stall, did a better job of securing her stall screen, and vowed to park around the corner from then on, out of sight.

Teeny enjoyed Rockingham, and I continued to send her out with a pony. One day, she ponied as usual, but when she pulled up past the wire and turned to come back, another horse galloped by too close to her. She jumped back and got loose. The minute she realized she was unattached, she took off, racing flat-out right toward the gap. I stood there helpless as she flew by, right off the track, and ran around the corner of the barn that was right there. I braced myself, waiting to hear the crash of her running into something, but nothing. And then, here came Aimee Hall on her pony, leading my notorious filly.

"Here's Teeny," Aimee said, a big smile on her face. "I saw her flying off the track, and I imitated you calling her and she screeched to a halt and let me catch her!" Once again, Aimee to the rescue!

Teeny was melodramatic, to put it mildly. You never had to wonder what she liked or didn't like. People were high on the list of "didn't like," of course. We were very lucky that Tom Schwigen had let her deal with the starting gate by herself. She was so small that she'd walk into the gate as readily as she would into a stall; she'd stand perfectly, eyes focused on the track in front of her, and break quickly. She knew her job; she didn't need an assistant starter holding her. Late in the fall of her three-year old year, she ran again, back at Suffolk. She was her usual tough self in the paddock, and I stood in my usual spot watching her warm up. Then, when the horses filed behind the gate to begin loading, I heard an announcement: "Due to Land will be fitted with blinkers." What?? I ran to the scale house and called the stewards. They confirmed that the paddock judge had noticed a notation in her past performance indicating blinkers. I assured them that it was a mistake: I didn't even have my set of blinkers at the track! She'd never worn them in a race. Fortunately, the stewards listened, and quickly watched a film of her previous race, but in the meantime, behind the gate, the starters had grabbed her and put a set of blinkers on, which, knowing Teeny, was not easy to do. Once the stewards had decided I was right, they took them off, and loaded her. The race went off, and she ran, but very disappointingly. When she returned, I could tell she was in a snit. We took her back to the barn, gave her a bath and I noticed something ominous: she had "the thumps." The vet came right over and treated her, and she managed to recover quickly, but it was obvious that all that wrestling before the race had upset her. Her three-year old campaign ended on a sour note.

She never got the thumps again, but another problem surfaced: her knee. Teeny never did anything halfway and galloping was no exception. She went around the track in attack mode, thundering along which made me send her out ponying so many times. Now, though, all that aggressive movement was taking its toll on her knees, one in particular. I did the usual race-track palliative care: sweats, bandaging and then, why not whirlpool? Macho loved his sessions in the whirlpool boots, why not Teeny? Well, everyone in the barn who'd watched her in action thought I was crazy. She would never tolerate that, right? Wrong! If nothing else, Teeny was smart. She'd watched Macho on a daily basis standing there happily while the water roiled around his legs. I approached her carefully with the boots, and she was guarded but cooperative. She stepped in, one leg and then the other, then stood while I poured hot water slowly around her, and then turned on the motor. She didn't move. So, I added a whirlpool session to my schedule. Now, every day after training, Macho had his hour in the boots, and then Teeny. She was even better than he was. After a few days, I could go to the track kitchen for coffee and leave her there, and she'd still be standing motionless when I got back.

All the pampering held off the inevitable, but by spring I knew she'd have to either retire, or have her knee attended to. Retirement? She was only four, and she was not a candidate to be retrained as some pleasure horse, so off she went to Tufts.

Dr. Kirker-Head scheduled her for knee surgery, but she'd barely arrived at the hospital when I got a call: he suggested postponing the surgery. He said she seemed agitated, and they'd like to wait a few days until she settled down. I assured him that "agitated" was her default mode: just do it! I drove out the next day and sat in the observation room while he removed chips from the troublesome knee. The surgery went well, and when they moved her to the padded recovery stall, I watched as she got to her feet. This was often a scary moment and many horses tried to stand before they were ready, and flailed around. Not my little genius. She sat up, and you could see her thinking. We waited and watched; minutes went by, and then she took a deep breath, and stood up, steady on her feet, no flailing. The attendants fitted her with a bib to keep her teeth from the bandage and as they were adjusting it, I went to her and tugged gently on her forelock. She was still very groggy and her eyes were all swollen from the pressure of lying on the operating table, but she felt my touch, and quietly nickered to me.

The operation was deemed a success. We decided to take her to the farm to recuperate. I'd planned to leave her at the track, the way we did with Macho, but my vet insisted that she should be turned out in a small area, so we did bring her home. I kept her in a stall for a week, taking her out in a quiet moment and hand-walking her up and down the aisle, but she was very wound up. Finally, I decided to take the vet's advice, and walked her out to the lunging ring. That was a small space; it was also flat, free from rocks, and fairly soft. I walked her around a few times, which wasn't easy. It was like walking a loaded grenade. Finally, I turned her loose. She stood for a few seconds, made a circuit at a nice trot, and just when I thought this would work, she exploded. She managed to run around that ring so fast that her shoulders had dirt on them, and the whole time she was running, she was screaming, a guttural, primal cry like some demonic goat. A few days of that, and we brought her back to the track. Amazingly, she seemed no worse for the wear.

We phased her back into training without further incident, and gradually increased her gallops. Spring turned to summer, and we all moved to Rockingham. The warm weather toned her down considerably. Greg Knight, who had been so good at galloping Macho, offered to take her on, too. Even though he was tall, he was slim, and he humored her perfectly. She was still her opinionated self, though. She did not like most people and did not like noise. One day we were coming off the track, and as we walked to the barn area, my friend Dennis Wallace was walking toward us, along with one of his horses. His exercise rider saw us coming and yelled, loudly, to Greg: "Hey, Greg! Is that one of those Massbreds?" Before we could even react, Teeny pinned her ears and launched herself right at him. His horse wheeled, he hung on by one toe, Dennis dove for cover. Greg? He sat deep in the saddle and just laughed.

Finally, in August, I entered her in a race. It had been nine months since she'd run last. Once again, we enlisted Bill Klinke for her. He suited her perfectly, and even though he had to be careful dodging her teeth and her heels, he enjoyed her. Rockingham! One August day at Rockingham twenty-six years earlier, we won our very first race with our first homebred; now we were hoping to win another one.

Teeny is all business, but Bill Klinke hears us cheering them on.

Robbie brought her to the paddock for me, and Greg walked with us. It was a typical Rockingham Park day: very warm, bright and sunny. The paddock was shady, though and she was fairly good about being saddled, but I had to walk down the ramp with her until she got to the track. Once there, she was all business. The race went off, and I held my breath as she ran down the backside. Into the turn, she was right with the leaders and then, down the stretch, she was on the outside, inexorably inching closer. Right before the wire, she pinned her ears and stuck her nose out, a winner!

To this day, I can remember the flood of euphoria. I have that win picture framed and hanging in the barn, and I can remember all the wonderful details. Greg was in the picture, and Robby, of course, and Billy, and the smiles were brighter than the sunshine. There is nothing like it!

That night, after she'd come back from the test barn and cooled out, I lingered in the barn. It was late, almost everyone had fed his horse and gone. Greg came by, and we stood around by her stall just talking quietly. I did her up, putting poultice on her front legs and knees, packing her feet with mud, wrapping all four legs. It was a beautiful summer night; life was good.

Due to Land racing at Rockingham, on her way to winning.
It was her first race back from knee surgery.

We stayed at Rockingham into the fall. Teeny went back to training after a few days' rest, with apparently no ill effects from her race. Her favorite treat was mints. I kept a jar right in the shedrow, and fed her whenever I wanted. One day, Greg came by after training. He took some mints, walked over to her stall, stuck his hand in, and she bit him. Bit him hard, bit through a good portion of his right hand ring finger. Greg spun away from her, writhing in agony, but even in his pain, he was understanding. "I broke her rule," he said, clutching his hand. "I didn't wait for her to stick her head out, I invaded her space." He went off to the emergency room for many stitches but he never said a bad word about her, although years later, when I ran across him on Facebook, he messaged: "Tell Teeny to spit out my finger!"

I'd felt her wrath, too. When she was just three, I was tacking her up in the stall, just putting the bit in her mouth. Dorothy came by to get on her, and instead of waiting for me to bring her out, stepped into the stall. Teeny whipped her head around, and the bit caught me in the side of the head, right above my eye. I gave Dorothy a leg up, and we set out for the track, but by the time we'd reached the gap, I could look up and see the swelling. It was quite a gash. I never got stitches, but the scar is still there. Teeny had her rules!

Back at Suffolk, she ran three more times that year. She seemed content enough, and still galloped with her usual vivacity, but once again, there were problems. Her knee seemed to be bothering her again. I always sent her to the track in white polo wraps, and when she came back, there was much less dirt on one heel than the other; she was definitely favoring it. The whirlpool seemed to keep things at bay, but I knew this was not going away.

In December, she ran again, with a new rider, Maureen Blanchette. Moe had finally decided to get her jockey's license, so the two were reunited again in the afternoon. Moe did a great job with her. She was quiet in the post parade, good in the gate, and burst out running. She was second on the backstretch, then made the lead at the turn. We were all cheering her on, knowing how tough and determined she was. I could see her thundering toward the wire, in front but as they approached, she gave way. At the end, three others stuck their noses in front of her.

I was concerned. Teeny was a competitive horse, and giving way in the stretch was not like her. She cooled out fine, but in the following days, I noticed a new issue: her tendon. The tendon on the leg opposite the one she'd had surgery on was getting sore. This was not good, there was no quick cure for tendons. Now, she was turning five. She stayed at the track for a few more weeks, but I knew this was just letting her unwind. She could go home and join her mother and grandmother in the pasture.

DUE TO LAND: 9 starts / 2 wins / 1 second

CATHOLIC CHARITIES

Due To Land

SUFFOLK DOWNS

School House Farm's
Susan Walsh, Trainer
William Klinke, Rider
6 Furlongs 1:15 1/5

Prosperous Tears 2nd
True Style 3rd
May 15, 1994
© Equi–Photo

SCHOOL HOUSE FARM OWNER
SUSAN WALSH TRAINER
WILLIAM S. KLINKE UP
PURSE $5,600

DUE TO LAND

ROCKINGHAM PARK

WATER STAR 2ND
FAIR MISS 3RD
6 FURLONGS 1:12:2
AUGUST 19, 1995
© 1995 HODGES PHOTOGRAPHY

Due To Shine (Shine)

When Macho and Teeny were yearlings, we bred both Lady and Duly back to Sunny. Lady was very cooperative for Sunny, as she always was, but she just couldn't seem to get in foal. We bred her through three cycles, and finally gave up. Maybe she was just too fragile at this point to carry a foal. Duly, however, caught almost immediately, so the following year, I was back on the foal watch.

This was Duly's second foal, so I knew it would be harder for me to time it to be there. Sure enough, her due date arrived, and everything seemed ready, but nothing happened. Then, another fruitless night. Then, I reasoned: she's waiting for me to leave her alone. When would that be? Not at night, when I was always popping in to check on her; maybe in the afternoon, during lunch. I waited until just after noon. Woody went into his house right on schedule, the farm employees congregated in the office with their lunches, and all was quiet. It was a bright, sunny day, sunlight pouring in the south-facing windows, and the door was open, so I could slip quietly in. I tiptoed to Duly's stall. She was standing, but as I watched, she pinned her ears, then shifted her weight, then walked in a small circle, then, stood. A minute went by, and she pinned her ears again, and swished her tail. Aha! I backed out of the barn and stood quietly outside for a minute, to give things time to get going. I remember this vividly: standing behind the barn in the sun, listening to birdsong, and then looking at the back hill. As I watched, I saw four big birds walking up through the grass. Big birds. Really big birds. Turkeys! That was the first time I'd ever seen a turkey on the farm. It was the beginning of an influx of these odd animals. Within a year or two, herds of them would be common, but that day, a rarity.

I thought briefly: I hope this isn't an omen of some kind. And then I snuck back into the barn. Now her labor was obviously beginning. How strange, right in the middle of the day, but it was unmistakable. Her sides were twitching, her tail was circling, and now she was flopping down in the straw. Bill Eldridge and Susan Donnely were coming back from lunch, and I had time to wave them over. They'd never seen a mare foal. The three of us just stood quietly outside the stall and watched.

This was about as picture-perfect a delivery as anyone could want. I didn't have to do anything, just observe. Duly was all business. Her contractions were strong, and each one advanced the foal along its journey. Within just a few minutes, she came slipping gently into the world. At that, I went in and cleared the caul from her head. Duly jumped up and started licking her dry, and the foal, another filly, looked around with huge, liquid eyes. When she decided to get up, it was smooth: no crashing up and down, but one smooth lunge that left her propped on her quivering legs. She was a beauty, too: a good size, dark bay with a small pretty star, beautiful large liquid eyes, and a little dish to her profile.

Due to Shine one day old.

I was still hanging around the barn admiring our newest when Jim drove home from work, so I called him over, and he agreed: she was a gem. He'd already been thinking of names, of course: Sunny Clips/ Duly Royal gave him Due to Shine! We applied to the Jockey Club and got that easily, but we kept on calling her "the baby" for a long time. Later, when Edgewood Farm became an up-and-running retirement facility, the huge main complex filled what used to be the lower hay field. Lots of the residents liked walking through the farm end on a daily basis. One was Herb Pinto, a wonderful man who came every day bearing carrots for the horses. Due to Shine was his favorite. He called her Babe, and she responded by always rushing to the fence when she saw him coming.

Our easiest birth soon morphed into our easiest foal, and then our easiest yearling. She never seemed to hit a snag. She was wonderful to work with, sweet-tempered and relaxed. When we weaned her, we began turning her out with Lady as a companion, and she settled right in with her. She was amazingly healthy. Unlike just about any other foal, she never got "scours" when the mare came into her foal heat; and she survived her entire first two years without a scratch. She grew into a beautiful yearling, too: a deep mahogany coat and a thick black mane and full tail. She didn't mind being handled, was relaxed when we first had her feet trimmed, didn't bite, didn't rear-and yet she was very athletic. She had a patented move when she was turned out: she'd run into the pasture, prop, then explode vertically, all four legs off the ground. She did this every day, so predictable that one day I brought my camera and caught it on film. Where Teeny could be exuberant to the point of violent, and had a dislike for just about anyone, Shine was exuberant in a happy, relaxed way, and was flat-out friendly. She never met a person she didn't like.

My life was frantic now, to say the least. I had horses at the track to train, so I got up at dawn, raced to Suffolk, got them all out to the track and then settled in afterwards, then raced through traffic to school to teach, then back home after that to take the horses in for the night. I'd been doing this for years, though, so I was used to it. I was always running late, of course, since you could never predict traffic or training problems. I often ended up shimmying out of my jeans at a stoplight and slipping on my school pants. One day, a bus full of sailors pulled up next to me in the middle of all that; it was a little awkward. Then there was the day when I raced to get to my first-period class, started giving a lecture at the blackboard, whipped out what I thought was a piece of chalk, and it was a carrot. In the midst of all this, Shine was getting older by the day, to the point where she needed to be trained.

One day, she and Lady were turned out in the small paddock behind the stud barn. I was watching from the door, contemplating how I could fit in her training. I walked into the paddock with an empty bucket, stood on it next to her, leaned over her and patted her off side, and then, while she just stood there quietly, swung up onto her back. She never moved. I did that for a few days when I had the time, then did the tack-up-and-walk-to-the-pasture method. I got on her a few times in the aisle of the big barn, tacked, and she was still calm about it. I didn't want to do more, though; since the farm had been closed, and all the boarders had gone, I thought breaking a horse by myself with no one around was just not a good idea.

Shine does her morning helicopter move.
Grandmother Lady is not impressed.

We turned this time to our friends the Ryans at Oakhurst Farm. They had been great caretakers of Sunny when he was there, had been very caring to Millie and O2B, and they had a nice setup for training. Their main barn was huge, with a big center aisle and stalls on either side, but around the perimeter of the whole structure was a wide track, so you could gallop even in bad weather. They also had a great added feature: Dennis Nobles. Dennis is, quite simply, a horse nut. He loves horses and loves to ride. He's now relocated to Kentucky, where he works with some of the superstars in the racing world, but at the time, he was at Ryan's farm, breaking youngsters. Once again I called on Joe Moore, and he arrived to bring Shine to them.

I had become very attached to this beautiful, sweet girl. I had ridden in the van with Teeny when she left home, but then I was afraid that, in her opinionated, reactive way, she'd dislike the experience and fling herself out a window. I didn't anticipate this with Shine, but I wanted to escort her on her maiden voyage, to delay her leaving. Joe agreed, so the two of us, with Shine in a nice box stall in his van, drove the hour or so to the Ryans. The box stall arrangement once again worked well. She settled herself in that space where she was comfortable, and rode quietly. We drove up right on time, and Dennis was there to meet us. I said my goodbyes, and she followed Dennis into the barn. He was at the track every morning, so he could update me then.

I always hated letting any of our horses out of my sight, but I had confidence in the Ryans' care and Dennis' expertise. The next day, I met him at Suffolk, and he had a big smile on his face. He told me that we hadn't even driven out of sight before he said to Patty Ryan, "Let's see what she knows," and tacked her up. He jogged her around the indoor track without a hitch.

It wasn't long at all before Dennis declared her broke and brought her to my barn at Suffolk. I'll never forget the first day she trained. Like all young horses, she went out late, just before the track closed for training, when it was quiet. Dennis was too busy to commit to me on a daily basis, but he'd offered to start her off for her first few days. I tacked her up, and we walked to the track. When we got to the gap, there was almost no one out there. I could see Cathy Chumbly, the outrider, sitting on her pony on the back side of the turn. Dennis and Shine trotted confidently onto the track and down the stretch, and I took up a spot on the rail.

I watched breathlessly as the two of them cantered past the grandstand, around the clubhouse turn, past the starting gate, and down the backside the whole time, nice and composed. No one would ever suspect that was her first day out there. Finally, they cantered by me and slowed down, preparing to pull up and walk off. By then, she was the only horse out there except for the vigilant outrider. Dennis yelled over to me, "Susan, watch how she can change leads!" Right there on the track, he cantered her in figure-eights, switching leads like a dressage horse. Cathy saw this with her hawk eye and yelled over, "Dennis! Cut that out!" A moment I will never forget. Horse number eleven had started.

Dennis got on her for me for the first few days, but then Greg took over. Greg loved galloping her and she moved so beautifully and effortlessly for him, that he took to calling her Serena's Song. After piloting the aggressive Macho and the unpredictable Teeny, Greg felt like he was on a Cadillac. I allowed myself to get very optimistic about her future. She was a pleasure to deal with, and so relaxed around the barn that I felt I could shedrow her myself when I needed to. She never bit, never kicked, never missed an oat; she was close to perfect. On the track, she was poetry in motion. She had a long, effortless stride, and never seemed to find anything remotely difficult. She got the dreaded gate card without any fuss, and she made my job easy. I started to think that maybe, just maybe, we'd finally got it right. We'd bred a horse who had ability, temperament, and soundness.

Shine's first day carrying weight.

She trained as a two-year old, spent that winter at Suffolk, and then, as a three-year old, started a series of breezes, heading to the day when she'd be fit and ready to run. Her training proceeded in a completely normal way, gradual increments of galloping, more and longer breezes. We moved to Rockingham for the summer, and she continued. I always sent her out in white polo wraps, and heads would turn when she breezed. Finally, I figured she might be just a breeze away from running. She was going to breeze five-eighths of a mile with Greg. Since it was a weekend, Jim came up to watch, too. Off she went, galloping down the stretch, and then, when she got to the backside, she slipped into a breeze: fluid, accelerating, reaching out with those long legs. I held my breath as she went by, people chatting by the rail stopped as she passed. When she came back, Greg had a big grin on his face. Jim went to meet them, ecstatic. Back at the barn, she cooled out quickly, and I gave her a bath, and then, my favorite time, when everyone else left, I did her up for the night, putting poultice on her legs, packing her feet, and just admiring this wonderful horse we'd bred ourselves.

The next morning, she was scheduled to walk. I took her out of the barn to wash off her poultice. It was a beautiful day, with an easy schedule. I took my time, enjoying the sunshine and hosing her legs. When I'd almost finished, I suddenly noticed something ominous: right in the middle of her tendon, a tiny bulge. This was a moment repeated hundreds of times in the horse world, the moment when you realize it's all over. I put her back in the stall and ran for the vet. She was dismissive, "Oh, you're overreacting. That's just the vein that runs behind the tendon." True, but why was it enlarged?

Greg and his girl Due to Shine at Suffolk.

Sure enough, the next day it seemed to be growing. The vet did an ultrasound and detected some damage. She was still shrugging it off, it wasn't that bad, I could back off on her training and jog her. Well, let's face it, people who breed horses are basically optimists, or they wouldn't even attempt it. The vet was giving me some hope, so I grabbed it. In my heart, I felt that it was over, but I did what she suggested. We backed off on her training, I poulticed and hosed, she jogged, and jogged-and yet I just couldn't make that barely-noticeable bulge go away.

We went back to Suffolk for the winter. Greg was optimistic and he either jogged or shedrowed her every day. At Christmas, he shedrowed her wearing a Santa Claus hat, and swore she felt great. In spring, Greg left the area, so I enlisted the help of Kenny Houghton, who was always in the barn galloping Tim Kirby's horses. He got along well with her, too, and we went back to easy gallops. Fortunately, she was well behaved and relaxed, so she was manageable at these slower paces. All this time, we continued the ultrasounds, constantly, looking for a time when everything would look perfect.

Soon, it was summer, and we were back at Rockingham. Miguel Santiago was galloping her now. He was also a jockey, so I could use him to breeze her. One day, we decided to let her go an "easy" three-eighths. Rockingham's track was not as deep as Suffolk's, so theoretically it would be easier on tendons. She had never taken a lame step in all this time, and the ultrasounds, if not perfect, weren't any worse.

Another beautiful day, ideal conditions. Miguel and Shine headed out, galloped around, and soon they slipped into a breeze. Someone standing next to me turned and said, as she sailed by, "WHO is this one?" It raised goose bumps on my arms. She breezed like a superstar. In a few minutes, she came jogging back. As they came toward me and off the track, I knew: this time, it was over. After all this time, after all the shedrowing miles, all the jogging, all the easy gallops, one notch up into an easy breeze, and it fell apart; she was lame. Not emergency /call the vet lame, but noticeably off. If she couldn't handle that easiest of breezes, there was no way she was going to make the races. It was hard to accept. She had no conformational flaws, no tricky feet like Duly, no glass knees like Macho, no mental glitches like Dansin-yet this was the one who never made it to the races. She had every quality we'd dreamed of, the complete package, but she was going home.

Due To Shine: Unraced

Timmy with his mother, Duly Royal,
and Johnny with his mother, Sunny Reign.

Duly's Dancer (Timmy) & Regan's Ridge (Johnny)

As easy as it had been to raise Due to Shine by herself, we still wanted to have foals in pairs, thinking of how Duly and Aggie had bloomed by having another foal to play with. We stuck to our vow never to breed a mare right back after she'd foaled, but when Shine was a yearling, Duly was available. We had retired Lady from the breeding shed, but we also had another young mare: Sunny Reign. She had a brief, impressive career, but developed a problem with her hind end, so we retired her.

Macho and Reign were full brother and sister, by Sunny Clips out of Lady. They were both big, strapping chestnuts like their father, and both could run, but Macho had inherited Sunny's powerful hind end, and Reign, unfortunately, her mother's weak one. She had a great attitude toward racing, and a beautiful big stride, so we thought it was worth breeding her.

Sadly, Sunny Clips was no longer my in-house stallion. He had developed EPM, a horrible, debilitating disease. By the time we bred him to Duly, the mating that resulted in Shine, it was becoming difficult for him to stand on his hind legs to breed. He'd lose his balance and weaken. The last time we bred him, Duly seemed to realize this, and she shuffled along with him, a macabre dance that, nevertheless, resulted in her foal. Sunny's condition slowly deteriorated, and when he became unable to rise and proved dangerous to himself, we reluctantly euthanized him. A wonderful horse, but he left only our four Thorougbreds to carry on. We decided to breed both Duly and Shine that spring, hoping for a pair of foals.

In the last few years, I had been in a barn at Suffolk with the Kirbys, a father-son operation from nearby Dover. Mr. Kirby had been breeding Massbreds for years, and always had his own stallion. He never advertised, but his stallion was always the leading sire in the state. His son, Timmy, had been working by his side since he was a little kid. They were dedicated, knowledgeable, and successful. Sharing the same barn day in and day out, in all kinds of weather, we had become good friends, and now that I had two mares I wanted to breed, I turned to them.

Their stallion at the time was Sundance Ridge, a tall, handsome dark bay with a wonderful disposition. Reign had actually met him before. Once when she won a race at Suffolk, she had to go to the test barn, and as she was walking in, Sundance Ridge, who'd won an earlier race, was walking out. The two looked each other in the eye, the proverbial two ships passing in the night. Now, she and her half sister went to the Kirby's farm in Dover for a closer encounter.

When any of our horses had to go to Kirby's, I never worried. Tim was an expert in handling his stallion and getting mares in foal, and he treated my horses like his own. They both had their visits, and both returned in foal.

Now, a year later, I once again began a foal watch. Duly's due date was before Reign's, and this would be her third foal. We planned to have her foal in the stud barn again, in the same stall which opened into the paddock. Once again, I watched. She had been so cagey with her second foal, going into labor in the middle of lunch break, that I was afraid she'd do this again, but I only had two nights of checking before she went into labor. She foaled early in the evening after we'd fed and settled everyone in for the night, but before the time I usually came back to check. Our house was so close to the barn that I could practically hear the straw rustling. I had that feeling that she was getting ready, went to check, and there she was!

Like her second foal, this third baby had a model delivery. Duly lay down in the straw, had some contractions, had some more powerful ones, and the little one appeared. A few more contractions, and he dove into the world. After two fillies, this one was a colt. Like Teeny, he was dark bay, almost black, but like Shine, he had a beautiful, refined head and a gorgeous, liquid eye. He was a knockout. Jim came over, and we had those wonderful few moments of bliss, watching our new foal and picking out clues of his future greatness. This time, Duly had no problems, and went right into her mothering role. It was a wonderful night.

The next day, we turned them out in the paddock. Once they were outside, away from the deep bedding of straw, we could get a better look at the foal. He was beautiful, a good size, nice proportions, and athletic looking, but in the light of day, we noticed a flaw: his left front leg. He had a nicely muscled forearm, a flat knee and then his lower leg stuck out at a serious angle. I noted that, then hoped that Jim would miss it, and just then, one of the boarders rode by on her horse. She stopped, smiled, and said, "Oh, what a cute little guy! Look how that leg just sticks out!"

Well, we did what we had done in the past, when Millie was down on her front heels, and Duly herself had a contracted left hind, and Reign was windswept: ignored it. I reasoned that being outside and running around would sort things out. Amazingly, in a week or so, his leg straightened out. By the time he had matured, his conformation was about as correct as you could want.

We kept the two of them over in the stud barn for two weeks. The farm was changing. The whole back acreage had been sold to a corporation that was going to build a retirement center, and there were plans for the road out back to be widened. It was going to cut right through the paddock, unfortunately. Woody wisely suggested to us that we use the back field, which wasn't in the new plans. To do that, we had to build a good fence across the top end, which we did. That gave us a beautiful flat pasture for our horses which would be away from all the new construction. It was very wet in the spring, however; so we left Duly and her foal where they were until it dried. It was easy to bring them out in the morning into the paddock, then across the back road and into the new pasture since the two gates were right across from each other. As soon as the ground firmed up, out they went. The new fence was, for us, expensive, but Woody had given us excellent advice. The horses could be turned out there without interference.

Jim was quite taken with our latest foal. He loved his looks, loved the way he moved, loved his friendly attitude. He came up with a name for this son of Sundance Ridge/ Duly Royal: Duly's Dancer. The Jockey Club accepted it, but it was a little ungainly for everyday use, so, in honor of Tim Kirby, we called him Timmy.

Timmy.

When Timmy was just a month old, Reign started showing signs of imminent birth, so we moved her into the stud barn. This was Reign's first foal, so according to my unsuspecting-mare theory, I thought I could manage to be there when she was ready to deliver. There were a few sleepless nights, but when she went into labor, I was there. I'm glad I was for this one especially. Reign's racing career had been cut short by hind end problems, and I was worrying about possible difficulty in foaling. She did well, though. It seemed as if it took forever, but with a little help on my part, her foal finally made his debut and it was an impressive one. This was by far the biggest foal we'd had. Reign herself was tall, maybe 16'2, and Sundance Ridge was over seventeen hands, so I guess we should have expected it, but when the foal got to his feet, and I was standing behind him steadying his hind end, his hips were higher than my elbows. There he stood, a tall, handsome chestnut, a colt, with a brilliant shine to his baby fuzz; and a broad white forehead that tapered down his nose, like a giant blazing torch. He was striking.

Yes, he did look good, but he flopped right back down in the straw and seemed lethargic. Not a good sign. Then, he just lay there. He didn't do the usual struggle to get up. After a few minutes, I was concerned enough to call the vet. Helen answered the call, and suggested we milk out Reign and make the foal drink. Well, Reign had never done this before, so we had a few tricky, uncomfortable moments, but eventually, I managed to get some milk into a cup, and then with an empty syringe, fed it to the foal. He had a good sucking reflex, thank God, and it worked like a charm, jump-starting him to getting up. At last, he stood. He was so gangly that I had to keep steadying his hips, but he finally started moving, then, nursing. This was very tricky, since a mare's udder is located in an out-of-the way place to begin with, and this foal was a lot taller than most. I thought of little Teeny as a foal. She just had to walk under Duly and raise her chin. This, though, required the foal to stand alongside, lower his head, then twist his nose up under her. Tricky! It seemed to take forever, and by the time he figured it all out, Jim and I were emotionally drained.

The next morning, we shuffled them out into the paddock. He was much stronger by then, and in spite of the length of those legs, he didn't have any obvious conformational flaws. Duly and Timmy were in the big back field, separated from the paddock by the back road, so Reign and Duly could see each other. The weather was cooperating, too, and his first day was spent in wonderful, warm sunshine. By the end of the day, he seem to have filled out everywhere, and even his initial gawkiness was fading.

That morning, when I got to the barn at the track, I couldn't wait to tell the Kirbys that another Sundance Ridge colt had arrived. Mr. Kirby asked what we were going to call him, so I couldn't resist. I said that since we called Duly's foal Timmy, we were calling this one Johnny. I then had a rare sighting of Mr. Kirby's wonderful, brilliant smile.

For his official name, we decided to honor a good friend of ours, Mark Regan. He had been the executive director of the Massbreeders, so I had become friendly with him then, and he was also a great lawyer who had done some work for us. The official name for Johnny, duly approved by the Jockey Club: Regan's Ridge.

Regan's Ridge nose to nose with our dog.

Johnny turned out to be a big, goofy, friendly foal. One day, he and Reign were in the small paddock, and I walked in. He immediately came jogging over, but tripped, falling to one knee. As luck would have it, he landed right on a small rock and the joint swelled. I hoped exercise would solve it, but the next day it was still there like an orange stuck to the front of his knee. After a few days, I consulted Doctor Orcutt. The options were draining it, which may or may not work, or wait and see. Once again, we chose the wait and see. He wasn't lame; it didn't bother him. It bothered me, though, and I'd check it every day to look for changes. Just when I was thinking of doing something about it, it suddenly disappeared, never to return.

We loved having two mares and foals. The two colts became fast friends, and spent the long spring and summer days racing each other around the field, while the two mares quietly grazed. The construction of the retirement farm out back was proceeding full steam, so there was a constant stream of construction vehicles roaring by. Out in the back field, though, all was tranquil. For these two, life was good.

When they were six months old, we weaned them, using the subtract-a-mare method we'd done with Duly and Aggie. Again, it worked well, with little separation anxiety. The two mares went back to the main barn, and were again turned out with Lady, and the two boys went on with their lives, racing each other around the field. The only drawback of that pasture was in the spring, the runoff of snow melt from the hill made it very wet. One day, I was at the gate admiring the two colts as they grazed when I noticed they'd acquired some friends: two ducks, swimming around in the puddles.

Just when we thought this was easy, we were reminded of the risks of raising young horses. I arrived home one day in perfect weather, and stopped at the stud barn to ready the stalls for the evening. I looked out the door at the pasture where the two colts were, and noticed that Timmy was standing right by the gate. It was a beautiful day. Johnny was grazing in the distance; why wasn't he with him? Then, I noticed what looked like a ripe tomato stuck to his knee. Odd. I walked over to the gate and was stopped in my tracks by the sight. Not a ripe tomato, but his whole knee, slashed open, bloody, and bulging.

I had a flashback to the day when I came home to find Millie wounded. I opened the gate and brought him back into his stall. He was very subdued, and I was afraid that the look in his eye was shock, so I quickly called for the vet. While I waited, I tried to keep him quiet. I held him in the stall, offered him hay, patted him on his favorite spot, and stared at the horrible carnage on his leg. There was a shred of skin hanging off one side, and the skin above and below his knee had pulled back, leaving a bloody bulge of tissue and gore. It was horrible, but at least I didn't see signs of a severed vein or artery.

Finally, I heard a car outside, and the vet came in. She was not, alas, Bob or Helen, but a vet new to the practice I'd never met before. Timmy was quiet, though, and I thought she'd be able to stitch him up without a problem. Wrong. She looked at the knee, immediately became tense, and raised her voice. In that small barn with a low ceiling, it was deafening. Timmy started to shuffle nervously and she raised her voice again. Then, she prepared some tranquilizer, raised her hand, and jabbed at his neck. The needle ricocheted through the air into the aisle. She raised her voice again. The situation deteriorated rapidly.

This was not good. Finally, when Timmy was completely frazzled, she gave up. I held him, she handed me various materials, and I somehow got the wound covered, first rinsing it off with saline solution, then bandaging. It was not pretty, but it would have to do, and once the vet had driven off, Timmy quieted down again. I never saw that vet again.

When Jim came home, he was distraught. Everything was covered up, so he couldn't see the extent of the damage, but Timmy was arguably the most perfect foal we'd had to date. Everything about him had raised our hopes, and now this. The good news: the bandages stayed on that night, and the next day I called the vet again. Dr. Orcutt came out and assessed the injury. He said that, at that point, I should just keep it covered and let it heal.

We tried to do just that. At first, we turned him out in the small paddock, and he was good about letting me change his dressing. My friend Carrie Rennie, who was a pharmacist, came up with some wonderful adhesive tape, and a spray that would undo the tape without wrenching, so every day I'd redo the bandages. After a few days, I could secure the dressing above and below with this wonder tape, secure enough to turn him out in the big field, so he and Johnny were reunited. We may have been upset at this development, but he was fine with it, going on with his life without a care for the huge white bandage that accompanied him.

I can't remember how long this went on, but it was quite a while. The bandage got smaller as it healed, of course, but it was a daily battle to encourage good healing and beat back the edges that wanted to heal too fast and create proud flesh. Heal it did, though. In the picture of him galloping at Rockingham as a two year old (page 215), on the right side of his knee, you can just see a small tear-shaped scar, the only trace of the whole incident.

When it came time for them to be trained, I turned once again to the Ryans, and their not-so-secret weapon, Dennis Nobles. I did almost no preliminaries with these two. There was never anyone around, now that the farm had closed, and I was very busy with the other horses. I just let Dennis do what he did so well.

Two year old Johnny learning the ropes from Dennis Nobles.

When Johnny was being trained down there, I made time one day to go visit. It was a nice day, so Dennis galloped him around the indoor track for a while, then rode outside in the sunlight. The Ryan's dog was milling around with them, chasing a ball. Dennis sat on Johnny and talked to me for a few minutes, then turned him and headed out, to a trail he'd made down the power lines. Off they went, at a relaxed canter, up and down the undulating hill until they disappeared, the dog racing behind.

No one would ever guess, watching that, that Johnny was a green two-year old. Well, I thought, if he doesn't show any ability at the track, he'll make a terrific field hunter.

Duly's Dancer (Timmy) and Rachel.

Like Macho and Teeny, Timmy and Johnny had grown up together, and then had adjoining stalls at the racetrack. It was always fun working with the two-year olds, and these were both well broke by Dennis. I had a new exercise rider, too: Rachael Walsh. She was from Maryland, and her father now ran the farm where we had sent Duly to be bred to produce Teeny. She was a show-quality rider, and she absolutely fell in love with Timmy, so his introduction to the track was amazing. She treated him like one of the Phipps' horses in Shug McGaughy's barn. Timmy was wonderful, maybe the best mover we'd had yet, and built close to perfection. He was Shine's half-brother, and since my stud had passed away, he and Johnny were both by

Tim Kirby's stud, Sundance Ridge. Johnny was outstanding in his own right. He was the tallest horse we'd bred, well over seventeen hands, and he had a bright chestnut coat with lots of chrome (from both his mother, Reign, and her sire, Sunny).

The two settled in to the track routine. They both enjoyed the activity in the barn and the long gallops on the track. When summer came, we moved once again to Rockingham. Rachael was getting very busy. She didn't want to give up the mount on Timmy, but she asked me to find someone else for Johnny. I turned to Jackie Falk, who was a trainer and rider, but was willing to take on Johnny, too.

Timmy was the more precocious of the two. He quickly became competitive in his gallops, and started breezing. He started getting attention from onlookers, too. He was very mature looking and professional, even as a two year old. In Chris Robey's picture of him galloping at Rockingham in the morning with Dennis Nobles riding, he looks like an older, winning horse. When he went to the starting gate, he figured it out almost immediately. Rachael told me he'd walk in and stand, stare straight ahead, and listen for the little click when the gates were released, a smart horse. By the time we left for Suffolk in the fall, he already had his gate card.

Duly's Dancer with Dennis Nobles.

Timmy trained well all fall, and soon it was winter. He seemed to handle the winter track, too. Time flew, and he turned three. In February of that year, he made his first start. I named Harry Vega to ride. I didn't know Harry, but he'd approached me one morning, saying that his wife told him I had the best looking horse on the grounds. Flattery, maybe, but he got the mount. We trudged up to the paddock. Nancy Shina, who was in my barn, ran him for me, and he was very well behaved. In the paddock, I saw the track owner with his entire family, all dressed up. They had a horse who was favored to win, and they were ready! I stood in my usual spot and watched the race. Timmy broke alertly, and got the lead. Every time a horse inched his way up to him, he let out a notch, and down the stretch, he battled as two others challenged him. I was standing there screaming, of course, and suddenly realized that the track owner was standing next to me. He looked at me and said, "Is that your horse?" I smiled meekly, as he flashed across the wire in front.

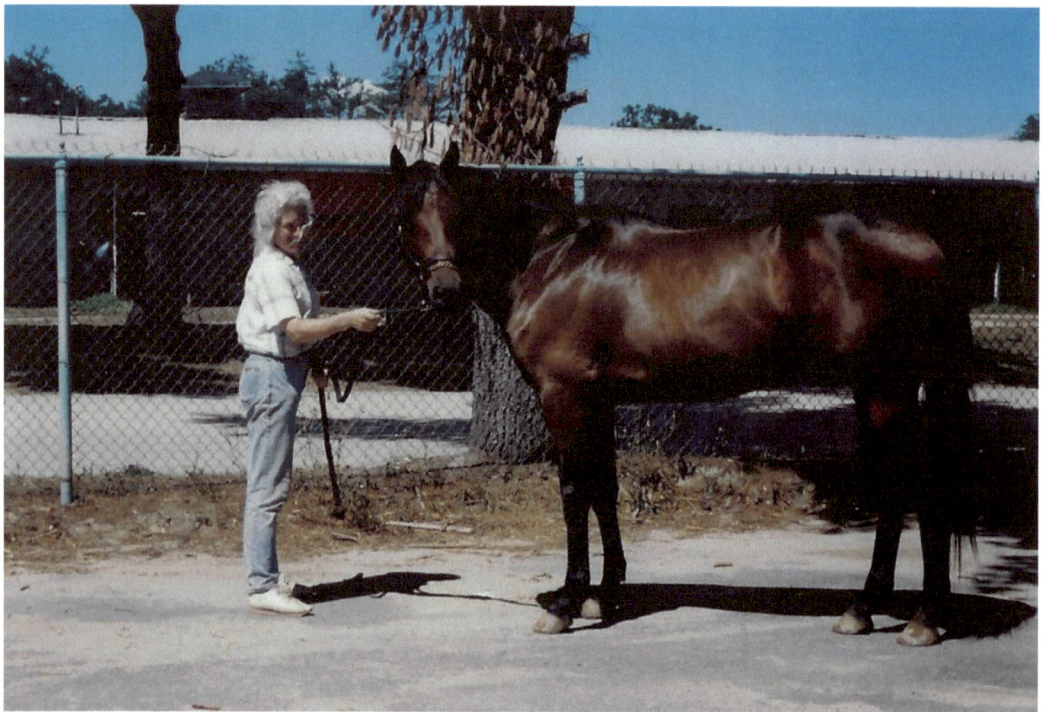

Two year old Timmy at Rockingham.

It is always fantastic to win a race; but to win a first start is very, very special. We were delirious, of course. My friends from the farm, Carrie and Denise, who'd been there when Macho won his first start - were there, too; and Carrie's parents. Once again, I felt that euphoria that only comes from winning a race, a feeling like no other.

The racing gods can be cruel, though. When Timmy went back to galloping, I was not happy with how he was going. Rachael thought he felt fine, but he just didn't seem to be striding out the way he had been. He ran two more times, and was disappointing. We finally sent him to Tufts to be scanned. I was afraid he might have some hidden, insidious problem like Teeny's tibia fracture. At Tufts, they found nothing. The vet even said that for a horse in race training, he was amazingly trouble-free. We finally decided it might be a deep bruise in his foot that just didn't show; so we backed off his training for a bit. Then, at Rockingham that summer, he seemed to come back to form.

We were optimistic about his Rockingham debut. He'd been training strongly, and we thought whatever had bothered him had been resolved. Harry Vega wasn't available, though; but we did get Rudy Baez to ride him. Rudy had won races on his mother and his grandmother and we had the pictures to prove it. On a beautiful summer day in New Hampshire, I stood at the edge of the paddock and watched him load into the gate. At the start of the race, he got an easy lead, and just as I was thinking he was back to his old self, he came to the turn, and I could see him bear way out, way out and suddenly the rest of the field passed him. When he straightened for home, he started making up ground, and finished strongly, but it was a bizarre performance, to say the least. Rudy had nothing to offer when he pulled up so the whole race was a mystery.

He ran again at Rockingham, this time with Jose Caraballo, who had done so well with Reign and Macho, but again, it was disappointing. He just seemed to fizzle. He lacked that edgy aggressive attitude we'd seen before. Then, after I hosed off the poultice on his legs the next day, another heart-stopping discovery: his tendon was inflamed.

Tendons! I had a flashback of the long, torturous fading of our hopes with Shine. Her tendon had started in just this way. Teeny, too, now back at the farm. Now, this didn't look good. This time, I didn't want to do any palliative measures; we just stopped training. Period.

In the spring, we thought the tendon issue was resolved; he seemed to be training fine. Harry Vega was back, too, so in the three races he was in that spring, he was the pilot. Again, though, we were disappointed. The first two were mediocre. In the third, he did show more speed, but didn't maintain it, and after that race, once again, the reason surfaced: his tendon. This time, there was no doubt in my mind. This was career-ending.

Timmy was perhaps one of our most disappointing horses. He had no quirks to overcome like Macho's feet or Dansin's stall-walking. There was nothing about him that should have limited him. He had the ability, as he'd shown in winning his first start, and his conformation was perfect, no flaws to indicate potential weakness. Yet, here he was, heading home. A sad day for us all.

Duly's Dancer: 8 starts / 1 win / 1 third

School House Farm's
Susan Walsh, Trainer
Harry Vega, Rider
6 Furlongs 1:13 3/5

Duly's Dancer

SUFFOLK DOWNS

Military Joe 2nd
Silver Swell 3rd
February 15, 1998
© Equi-Photo

And then there was Johnny. He was the tallest horse we'd every bred, well over seventeen hands. With his chestnut coat, blaze, and white legs, he was very much like his mother, Sunny Reign, and her father, Sunny Clips, but his height and legginess were from his sire, Sundance Ridge. He was a congenial soul. When Dennis Nobles broke him to saddle, he could ride him anywhere, and did. His favorite route on the farm was galloping down the power lines with a dog running alongside, not your typical two-year old.

When he was ready, he moved from the farm to Suffolk in the spring, and Dennis agreed to gallop him for us, to start him off. He took to the racetrack life quickly. He loved the activity around him, and enjoyed loping along in the wide open spaces of the racetrack.

Two weeks after he arrived, I was following Dennis to the track to see him train. He was so big and gawky that I was watching him walk from behind, always worrying about the possibility of his developing stifle problems, but when he got to the gap, he set off at a nice jog, and he looked good. I stood at the rail, right at the quarter pole, and watched him gallop around. He went by me, and the people I was standing with commented on his size, and how well he behaved. Then, they started down the stretch, and I stood where I could watch him galloping straight away. At the eighth pole, I thought he took an odd step. For a split second, he seemed to lose his rhythm but he continued on. Then, I stood in the gap and waited. Soon, he came jogging back toward me, but just as he and Dennis reached the end of the track itself, Dennis yelled over: "He did something to his stifle!"

I ran over and looked. He was definitely favoring a hind leg. We kept him going at a walk, right to his stall, and I hollered over to the vet. We unsaddled him right in the stall, and she came over minutes later. He was standing with his hind leg cocked and initially, she assumed it was a stifle. She said she'd come back in a while with her x-ray equipment.

I stood holding him in the stall. He was calm enough, but my mind was whirling. What now? How could I tell Jim that this horse was injured before he got started? He stood there looking at me, rather calmly, and I noticed he seemed happy enough just standing there, only showing discomfort when he put his foot down. The vet came minutes later, and I mentioned this to her. She slipped up beside him and felt his foot then looked over her shoulder at me with a horrified expression. "Oh, my God! I think there's a nail in here!"

Sure enough, she could just feel the tip of a nail, right next to his frog. It was a double-headed nail, so it was protruding just a tiny bit. A regular nail probably would have gone unnoticed, since it was in the side of his frog, not the groove.

There was no time to waste. We needed to send him to Tufts as soon as possible. Fortunately, my friend Joe Moore was on the grounds with his trailer, but in the few minutes it took to locate him, call Tufts, and bring the trailer around, Johnny's ankle was blowing up, and his pain was increasing.

I was on a first name basis with the receptionist at Tufts, which was not a good thing, but I was very grateful that it was there, and so close. Within an hour, he had arrived, been evaluated, and was prepped for surgery. It was what they call "street nail" surgery. X-rays had shown that the nail had penetrated the frog and gone right up into the tendon sheath, so there was no time to waste.

This was stunning. It was only his second week at the track, and he'd only had his hind shoes for a few days. I also knew exactly where it happened, right at the eighth pole, where I saw him take an odd stride. Dennis, who was there with him, agreed. How a nail managed to find its way to the track, how his hind foot managed to find that one nail, was beyond comprehension.

The next day, I went out to Tufts and watched their blacksmith fit him to a boiler plate: a shoe with a metal insert which covered his whole sole. Johnny stood there, his usual congenial self, while all this was taking place. Amazingly, his stay there was uneventful, and soon he was back at the track. We'd moved to Rockingham for the summer, and he settled right in.

The first time Jim saw his leg, he was horrified. When they'd done the surgery, they had used an arthroscope to clean out the tendon sheath, inserting it midway up his leg, so there was a lump there, and swelling and it looked like he was bowed behind. I had a tendon magnet which I'd put on his leg under his bandages and, amazingly, within a few weeks, it was back to normal. None of this seemed to bother Johnny. As long as he was fed and exercised, he was happy. He'd stand tied to the wall, while I worked on the leg. He never seemed to favor it. Wise horsemen, of course, would say this indicated that he had no talent. A good horse would have been ruined.

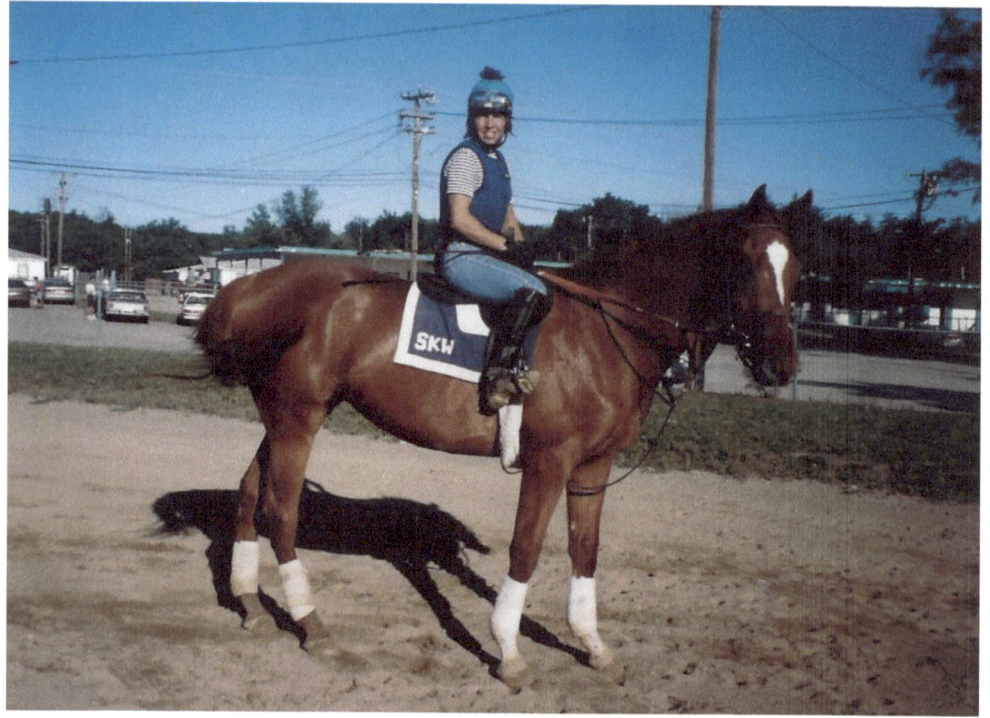

Johnny and Jackie Falk at Rockingham.

Once he was back to a regular schedule, I sent him to the gate. Although we'd started off on the wrong foot when Reign was doing her gate work, starter Tom and I had become good friends, so I sent Johnny over to the gate with Jackie, not worrying about it at all. After training, Tom came looking for me.

"Where'd you get that horse? My Lord! He looked like Man O'War coming over there! He's some old fashioned horse!"

Tom loved him. He completely enjoyed seeing him show up at the gate, and gave him his gate card without a problem. He did look like Man O'War, as a matter of fact, and his dam, Reign, was a direct descendant. Maybe…?

Little by little, his body and brain trained to the point where he was ready to run. By then, it was spring. Then, it was summer, and we went back to Rockingham. Finally, when we came back to Suffolk that fall, he was ready to be entered.

The first time he ran, Jose Caraballo rode him. He'd ridden Reign, Johnny's mother, and her full brother, Macho, so he had a great attitude toward this race. Johnny made an imposing impression in the paddock, too. He was so tall, so noble looking, that it was reminiscent of Man O'War. At this time, Timmy was struggling. Could this one turn our fortunes around?

Johnny was good in the paddock, albeit a little gawky. He marched down the ramp to the track, went right up to his pony, but when they started off, he was ebullient to a fault. He was plunging and leaping, like some giant chestnut dolphin, bounding along in front of the grandstand. Jose was not amused!

The race itself unfolded in the usual way, except for the dolphin running in the rear. He just didn't want to settle, plunging along. Jose was so horrified that he eventually wrestled him to a slow canter. In the chart of the race, he is listed as a DNF, the comment was "outrun."

We hoped that his performance was just due to greenness, but Jose wanted no part in a repeat. The next time he ran, Jorge Vargas was our jockey. Jorge was unflappable, competent, and always had a positive outlook. No matter; this time, the comment was "outrun." In his third start, he actually finished ahead of two other horses, but his performance was still dismal. Nothing about it gave us any encouragement. This time, it didn't take long for us to decide that his career was coming to a close.

As we walked Johnny back to the stable area, Tom Schwigen, the starter was standing by the rail. Tom had taken to Johnny from the start, but now he shook his head sadly and said, "Will you tell me how can a horse look *that good* and run *that bad*?"

Regan's Ridge: 3 starts / no placings

Sundance Land (Herbie)

When we were waiting for our thirteenth foal, our lives had undergone seismic changes. The farm was now completely closed. The retirement facility was up and running in what was the huge back hayfield, so our little house looked out upon this vast building now. The view to the front was still the same, all the farm buildings, but they were now all closed, except for the small stud barn, and our horses were the only ones left. The big barn stood locked and silent. My career had changed, too. I had stopped training, and was now a State Steward at Suffolk Downs, a job I'd never aspired to, really, but had come to love. There was one drawback: as a steward, I could not own a horse on the grounds, or even be the breeder of a horse on the grounds. Meanwhile, here was Teeny, retired from racing, still young and healthy, so, what to do?

Jim leading Teeny, Herbie leads the way.

Once again, we turned to our friends the Kirbys. Tim knew Teeny well, from being in the barn with her; and he knew that, although she was tiny, she had a huge heart, and loved the competition of the track. Her breeding was an interesting complement to that of his stallion, too.

Off she went, to be bred to Sundance Ridge and came back in foal. The plan was that once the foal was weaned, he'd go back to Tim, and he could race him. Teeny knew none of this, of course, and she knew nothing about having a foal, so once again, I was doing the foal watch on an unsuspecting first time mare.

Teeny was an interesting horse. She was small in stature, but had a huge amount of self-confidence. She did not like people, for the most part, and she was very reactive. She would rip around at a moment's notice, and was very bold. An example: when she, Lady and Duly were all out in the pasture one day, a boarder threw a blanket over the fence to air out. Lady and Duly immediately went to the far end of the pasture. Teeny? She saw this odd thing and immediately charged over to investigate. To tell the truth, she was one of my favorites.

Herbie with his great grandmother, Lady, and grandmother, Duly.

Now, all systems were go. It was a quiet evening, and in the stud barn, we'd filled her stall with fresh straw. I had dinner, then went over to check on her and on a hunch, went back an hour later, and she was starting to sweat up. This time, I got Jim, and we both watched quietly as her labor began.

Now, Teeny was small, but in no way puny. She had a very stout little body. When the contractions started, in typical Teeny fashion, she went for it and in minutes, a foal appeared. I slipped into the stall and peeled the caul off over his head. He was just half-born: head, neck and front legs were out, the rest still off stage, but as soon as the caul was off his face, he raised his head and whinnied lustily. Jim and I both laughed, and I said, "How healthy is this little guy?" One more contraction, and he was out.

Teeny was on her feet immediately, worrying over this little guy. He was a tiny colt, all dark like her, but with a huge white forehead that looked like a headlamp. That was a surprise.

Teeny was all motherly, hovering around him, licking him, but suddenly we noticed that this foal that we'd thought was so healthy was way too passive. It wasn't all that late, so Jim went back to the house to call the vets, and I set about milking out Teeny, thinking that this guy might respond the way Johnny had to a quick slug of mother's milk. That helped somewhat, but he was still way too lethargic. He didn't seem to care about getting to his feet at all. Well, we cared, so with some serious encouragement, we managed to get him up, and by the time Helen arrived an hour later, he'd managed to find the all-important udder. Teeny was wonderful with him, fortunately, and he was small enough that he could nurse without going through the contortions that a big foal like Johnny had to do. Helen looked him over carefully, of course, and determined that, although he wasn't a classic "dummy" foal, he was "in the spectrum," as they would say today. That made it very important that we make sure he got up to feed regularly.

It was a long night. By dawn, he could get up without our help, but he wouldn't do it on his own. It was almost as if the thought just didn't occur to him. If we were there to assist, though, he could stand up and nurse, so we basically just hovered around.

The next day, we were doing just that, hovering around, when we heard a car drive up to the barn. It was Doctor Bob Orcutt. We hadn't called him, but he said Helen had mentioned her visit last night, so he was just dropping by to see how he was doing. We were so blessed to have such caring veterinarians. His advice was the same as his sister's: just make sure he feeds the way he should.

It took a few more days of hovering around before we felt good about it. He did seem to sharpen up a little more every day, and by the end of the week, he seemed fine. An interesting note: there have been recent studies at U Cal/Davis about "dummy foals," and a possible link to autism in children. They theorize that the process of being born itself, of being squeezed by contractions in the way along the birth canal, is vital to proper development, and "dummy foals" have had deliveries that were too short, lacking the necessary squeezing. He certainly fit that model.

Four Generations: Lady, Duly and Teeny with Teeny's foal Herbie (center).

We turned them out in the small paddock right outside their stall, and soon the Edgewood residents came by to admire the new foal. One of the most regular visitors was Herb Pinto. He had fallen in love with Shine when she was turned out, calling her Babe, and now he came every day with carrots for Teeny and pats for the foal. One day, he asked what we were going to call the new one, and I said, "Well, we think we'll call him after his best friend. We'll call him Herbie!" Mr. Pinto was stunned to silence, then mumbled, "I'm going to tell my wife," and raced off, overcome with emotion.

It would be Herbie. Jim's formal name for this son of Sundance Ridge/Due to Land would be Sundance Land, but Herbie soon became a local star. Herb Pinto came to see him every day, usually with friends in tow. It was a pleasant walk from the retirement facility to the pasture where Herbie was, so there was a constant stream of visitors. We were very lucky with this foal. The weather was wonderful, and after his slow start, nothing went wrong. Jim and I were both very busy with our respective jobs, so after we'd turned them out in the morning, the horses were on their own. When it came time to wean, we sent Teeny and Herbie to the Kirby farm, and Teeny returned alone. The next spring, I brought Teeny down there again to be bred back to Sundance Ridge, and I got a chance to see Herbie, now a yearling, out in their huge pasture with two others. The Kirbys called them the "three amigos." It was bittersweet for me. I was glad to see him thriving, but sad to think how little I meant to him. After being hands on with all our other foals, this was a new experience for me. The following year, when he was at the track, I was no longer on the backside, but up in the stewards office all morning, keeping my distance, dissociating myself from him. It was hard.

Sundance Land: Did not start

Party Pants (Betty)

Teeny was in foal again. Surprisingly, she was well behaved when being bred. She seemed to like Sundance Ridge, anyway; and Tim Kirby knew her well from the track. Her first foal, Herbie, was with Tim at the track, but had yet to race. Now, in spring, she was ready to foal once again.

The farm was quiet now. Even though the huge retirement center was up and running, the fields we used, and the little barn, were not affected, except for the traffic streaming by the small paddock. We had several residents who were dedicated purveyors of carrots to our horses, and an increasing herd of turkeys, but our horses were the only equines on the whole property.

Now, Teeny's time was at hand. Since this would be her second foal, I wondered if she'd get devious, and wait it out until I wasn't around, but everything went right on schedule. I don't think I lost any sleep over this foal. The signs were there, the day drew to a close, the night settled in, and she went into labor. I was there, but she didn't seem to mind, and once again, she bore into her contractions and very quickly produced her second foal.

No giant white forehead on this one. She was a filly, but arrived with an impressive set of muscles. She was much larger than Herbie, too, and soon managed to struggle to her feet and stagger around in the straw. Once again, we had the nerve-wracking attempt at nursing, and once again, just as we thought she'd never figure it out, she did. We stood by admiring the tableau of mare and foal in the soft light.

The next morning, we turned them out in the small paddock right outside the stall door. There, with no deep bed of straw, we could get a good look at her, and we were pleased. She had "correct" limbs, and an amazing, strong and muscled body. She was also alert, staring through the fence at the cars driving by. Our only concern was her breathing, which I thought was much too rapid. I remembered Dansin when he was born, and how it took a few days for him to stabilize. She didn't have a temperature, which was good, and when the vet arrived to check out the two of them, he thought if we just kept her quiet, she should come around.

For the next two days, the two of them went out into the side paddock, which was full of nice, lush spring grass; but we kept Teeny on a shank, so that the foal wouldn't have to chase after her. That was fine with Teeny, and the foal still got exercise running around her like a little satellite. Sure enough, after two days, she was fine.

Now, the name. Jim deviated from his usual plan of using both parents' names. He had recently watched a series of lectures on PBS by Loretta LaRoche, and really enjoyed them, so he decided to use one of her phrases, Party Pants. Party Pants? Jim loved the name, and was looking forward to seeing her run and having Larry Collmus, who was the announcer at Suffolk, have fun with it. That name was fine with the Jockey Club, so Party Pants she would be. For her barn name, though, we turned again to her fan club. Herb Pinto had loved having us call Teeny's first foal Herbie, and we had become good friends with another resident couple, Jim and Betty Ruf, so this foal would be known to one and all as Betty.

Jim and Party Pants (Betty).

Betty had a wonderful childhood. Eventually, she went out in the big field with her mother, grandmother, and great-grandmother. Three of the four had been born right here, and we now had four generations grazing together. Being a filly, she was tolerated by all three mares, and had long, lazy days in the field to grow and mature. She was definitely Teeny's daughter. Although much bigger, she had that same boldness. She didn't like to be patted or gushed over, and she was very reactive. Just like Teeny, if she saw something out there that was odd, she'd charge right over to investigate.

One beautiful morning, when she was only three months old, I turned them out as usual. I led them out of their stall into the small paddock, then through the outside gate across the small farm road and into the big back field. I also had just "borrowed" a mare from Tim Kirby. I had the thought of breeding an Irish Sporthorse and raising it for myself, so Tim let me take another Sundance Ridge mare, She's a Trip. Obviously, he couldn't breed her to his stallion, who was her father, so he let me borrow her to breed to an Irish Draft stallion. She had arrived the night before, so on this particular day, I turned Betty and Teeny out in the back field, then went back and turned Trip out in the paddock. It was such a nice morning that I decided to sit for a while on the bench we'd set up beside the road, just to relax and enjoy watching the horses.

Trip walked over to her fence and stared over at the mares. Immediately, Betty spotted her and came over to her fence. The two looked at each other across the road, and Betty craned her neck over the fence to get a better look. They were tantalizingly close, but the road was just wide enough to keep them from touching. Betty stretched her neck again, and then, very calmly, she backed up, turned around, made a nice circle at the canter, and then launched herself right over the fence into the road. That fence was a good four feet high. I jumped up at once and ran over. She paused a minute, just long enough for me to open the pasture gate and shuffle her back in. Jim was over at the house, and he'd seen the whole thing, too. We were grateful that I'd happened to be right there, and at that point Betty realized that the new horse wasn't worth all the fuss. She never did that again. No harm done, and we thought that, if she didn't pan out as a race horse, she could always be a jumper!

Betty's first six months went very well. Having Teeny as a mother could be stressful. Sometimes something would set her off, and she'd tear around the field screaming. Betty was very philosophical about these moments. One day, they were in the big ring, which was now all grassed over, and Teeny started racing around the whole ring, hollering like a deranged mule. Betty stood in the middle, watching, with a look on her face like "there you go again!" When it came time to be weaned, she accepted that well, too. The winter set in, and she handled that as well. She was physically very robust, and it seemed as if she was mentally stalwart, too.

Before I knew it, she was a two year old. Old enough to be at a race track. Old enough to be trained. Now, what to do? Problem one. There was no way she could run at Suffolk Downs without causing a conflict of interest with my job. Problem two: where to send her for training. My two previous go-to people for readying horses for the race track had left. Dennis Noble had gone to Kentucky and John Hall had closed his farm and moved to Kentucky, too. The training problem had a simple solution. I started her with the tack up and walk to the pasture technique I'd done in the past. That seemed silly; but it made her totally relaxed with tack on. Then, I turned to a local horseman, Chuck Patti. At first, friends thought that an odd choice. His facility was only one town away, but he was known as a western/ paint trainer, not a Thoroughbred person. I reasoned that the key here was his expertise. He was respected by all as an excellent horseman, and I thought the Western style of training would give her a calm start. The racing part could take care of itself. I talked to Chuck, and he agreed not only to take her on, but to come and get her.

The day arrived. Chuck drove up with his truck and trailer, lowered the ramp, and introduced himself to Betty. We walked out of the barn into the stable yard where the trailer was, and she immediately froze. The farm had become so deserted that a truck/trailer behind the barn was a huge anomaly. Within minutes, I realized that my decision to send her to Chuck had been a good one. He took charge immediately, very quietly, but firmly. I stood by and watched as she came around to accepting him and following his lead, and in a reasonably short time, walked onto the trailer. As they drove off, she whinnied, of course, and I had to fight the lump in my throat that was probably the same struggle every mother felt when her little girl left for her first day of school. I knew I'd made the right choice, but I'd miss her.

I resisted the urge to make the short drive to Chuck's barn, figuring that her training would be smoother without my hovering around to distract her. A few days after she left, Chuck called with an update, "Betty's tough." Well, she was. Like her mother, she was not a cuddly kind of horse, and she was just as strong, too. The move from our barn to Chuck's had to be difficult for her. She'd led an unusually sheltered life. Since the farm had closed, I was the only person who handled her, and aside from the occasional retirees who visited with carrots, and visits from Jim, she had little contact with humans. She was in the same stall where she'd been born, and turned out in the same fields she'd known all her life. Now, even though Chuck's barn was only a few miles away, to her it might as well have been another planet.

Chuck said she was progressing, but she was a challenge. Tacking her up was the only thing she didn't seem to mind. He was able to work with her, however, and in a few weeks, he was riding her without a problem. Then, I got another call: she'd had an incident in her stall.

She was in her stall at Chuck's, when one of his helpers was filling water buckets. At home, I did them by hand. At Chuck's, the girl went from stall to stall with a hose. Apparently, she usually did this when Betty was turned out, but that day, Betty was standing right there. When she put the hose into the bucket and pulled the trigger, the sound of the water blasting into the bucket startled Betty, and, Betty, being her reactive self, flew back and slammed into the back wall, actually punching a hole in it. The place where she hit, on the upper side of her rear just behind her hip bone, swelled alarmingly. Chuck had Doctor Orcutt look at it later. He said it was basically a giant hematoma, and would probably resolve. "A long way from her heart."

The next day, I drove over to see for myself. She was out back in one of the turnout pens, and when I walked over, she came to the fence, looking her old self. Then, she turned and there, on her rear, right behind her hip bone, was a huge wobbling mass. It looked like someone cut a football in half and plastered it on her side. It was hideous.

Chuck had seen me drive up, so as soon as he'd finished with the horse he was working with, he came over. He said once again that it didn't seem to bother her at all, BUT he'd like to send her back home earlier than we'd planned. He felt that she was broke, but he worried about some of the women who were boarding there. They were convinced that she needed cuddling. One of them was doing that one day, and Betty tore the whole sleeve off her sweatshirt. He didn't want any of his boarders getting hurt.

This was fine with me. I still hadn't finalized the next step, so if he could bring her back, I could work on that hideous hematoma. Shortly, Betty returned to the same stall where she'd been born, and I sent Chuck off with a nice Breeders' Cup sweatshirt to replace the one she'd destroyed.

Betty loved being home, of course. She went right back to the pasture as if she'd never left. Jim was horrified when he saw the hideous hematoma, but I found that I could iron it and reduce it in size. I'd fill a plastic water bottle with hot, hot water, and when Betty was lying in her stall resting, I'd go in and just roll it over the hematoma, working from the outside in. Betty seemed to love this spa treatment, and in a matter of a few days, it was gone.

Now, we had a two year old, broken to ride. What next? I contacted Rachael Walsh. She had been my exercise rider when Timmy was at the racetrack. She was a superb rider, and she'd fallen in love with Timmy. I'd promised that when his career was over, she could have him, so he'd spent the rest of his life at a beautiful Maryland farm. She'd shown him with great success as a hunter and as a jumper, and even sent me a video of him in winter, with her riding bareback, cantering through the snow towing her brother on a toboggan. Now, she was training horses in Maryland, and she agreed to take Betty under her wing. After all, Betty and Timmy had the same father, and his mother was her grandmother. They were family.

It had been hard for me to send Betty away when she was going only to the next town. Now, Mark Choper's big van rumbled up the drive, and she loaded on, bound for Maryland, which, for me, might as well have been the moon. Jim and I stood forlornly in the yard while Mark marched her up the steep ramp into the van. There was another horse there to keep her company, and soon she was heading off down the drive. Foal number fifteen was on her way.

Our last two foals, Sundance Land (Herbie) and Party Pants (Betty) were the only two I didn't follow to the racetrack. Herbie spent his training years at Suffolk, but because of my job, I had to distance myself from him. I couldn't visit him in the barn area and couldn't watch him train. Betty trained in Maryland, way out of my range. After breeding horses, delivering them, starting off their breaking, taking them to the track and guiding them through to their retirement, I had to send these two off into the world on their own.

Herbie went to my friend, Tim, at Suffolk; Betty went to Maryland with Rachael. I saw them off the day they both left, but their careers unfolded completely out of my sight. I only know that neither horse had any serious physical problems, but neither horse made the races, either. How they did was, for the first time, out of my hands.

Party Pants: Did not start

Three Generations: Royal Stand, Duly Royal, Due to Land & Due to Shine.

CHAIN OF FOALS

PART II

Shine and her niece Betty living happily ever after at the farm where they were born.

After the Wire

All fifteen of the horses we bred made it to the racetrack. All of them went as two year olds, learned to gallop, practiced in the starting gate, breezed. All but four of them started in a race; nine of those who started won. We had sixty percent winners from horses bred, which is statistically very good, and two of those were multiple stakes winners. This was all done by a couple who thought it would be "fun" to raise a race horse, who had no farm of their own, who had no previous experience in racing. It was quite a ride!

Home from the track, Due to Shine made an easy transition from racing to trail riding.

A horse's racing career is, in the scheme of things, short. Most Thoroughbreds live to their mid-twenties, long after their racing days are over. What do you do with a used race horse? Here's what we did:

Sin Mill (Millie) in Texas with my niece, Anne Taylor.

Sin Mill: Our first foal. I retired her to the farm and rode her myself for a while, even going on organized trail rides. She had two foals (Penance and Sunny Crime). After that, we sent her to Austin, Texas, where she lived as the beloved pet of my niece, Anne Taylor. She lived a long, healthy life, but she died suddenly at 32.

Petrifier: I rode him at the farm myself for a while, but when it got to the point that I never had the time, I sold him to a nice young girl from nearby New Hampshire as her riding horse.

He's Dansin: We never did geld him. When his racing career was over, I saw an ad for a stallion wanted in the Chronicle of the Horse. The people came to look at him and immediately whisked him off to Michigan, where he lived happily, siring pleasure horses and a few race horses, too.

Agatha C: I sold her right off the track to Laura Kniffen from Rowley, who rode her for pleasure. The pair won the Vermont 100 Mile Rookie award, the first Thoroughbred to do so in many years. When I told a friend at the track about it, he said, "Well, you always thought she should go long!"

Duly Royal: One of our favorites, she never left us, having three foals, and then living a dignified retirement. She survived surgery for a leiomyosarcoma when she was seventeen, and she passed away in her twenties.

Sunny Crime: O2B joined his mother at my niece's place in Texas, and lived happily ever after.

Penance: I thought this would be my easiest rehoming. I gave him to a friend who'd begged me to let her have him when he retired. I did, but she in turn gave him to someone who neglected him. He was rescued by a group in Maine, and lived at their facility for the rest of his life.

Sunny Stand with some friends.

Sunny Stand: I rode him at home briefly, then loaned him, briefly, to a local equestrian. He did not respond well to her discipline, and quickly returned. I then loaned him to a wonderful woman, Liisa Jackson, who had him for the rest of his life, making him a local icon, a neighborhood pet, and a beloved member of the family.

Sunny Reign: I rode her a little myself, and then found yet another wonderful person who wanted to lease her, Andrea Mirarchi. She built a barn for her and loved and cherished her for the rest of her life.

Due to Shine back home learning the trails in winter.

Due to Shine: She came back to the farm and immediately converted to my riding horse. We had many riding adventures, venturing forth with my sister, Ellen, and her Morgan to local parks or the beach. In her later years, she developed Cushing's disease, but responded well to medication. Then, suddenly, as she was approaching twenty-one, I found her in the morning with colic-like symptoms, which quickly proved fatal.

Due to Land: She's still with us. With her theatrical personality and diminutive size, I thought she'd be best kept close to home, where she is to this day. She's twenty-nine and the feistiest horse we have.

Duly's Dancer: When his tendon problem ended his career, Timmy came home. For a few weeks, I turned him out in the small paddock behind the stud barn where he'd been born, with his leg wrapped in an elastic bandage. When he'd settled down, I turned him out in the big field with his friends. A year later, almost to the day, you couldn't tell which leg had the problem. Off he went to Maryland, to Rachel, his devoted and talented exercise rider. With her as his pilot, he had a stellar career in both hunters and jumpers, and spent the rest of his life as her father's stable pony at the beautiful farm he managed, Merryland. Timmy even made a cameo appearance in the book of the same name.

Regan's Ridge: A friend of mine who often deals in hunters sold Johnny for me to a woman in Virginia. When Bob Beauvais, the van driver, delivered him, he reported back to me that he was in the lap of luxury. I never heard any more from the people who bought him, but I have to think that with his size and his laid back attitude, he would have made a great and handsome field hunter.

Sundance Land: Herbie went to the track with Tim Kirby. When he didn't work out there, a friend of Tim's took him to New Hampshire for a riding horse.

Party Pants: Betty went to Maryland for her training, but never made the races. She came back to us as a four year old, and she's with us yet, possibly our greatest underachiever. She is turned out every day with her mother, and accepts carrots and apples from the residents of the retirement home. She and her mother have also appeared on the home's website.

The Cast of Characters

Many, many people are involved in developing a racehorse. Here's a list of some of the ones who had major roles in our horses' lives: exercise riders and jockeys (*).

SIN MILL:
Guy Henry
Brent Kelly*

PETRIFIER:
Tony Barreira*
Henry Ma*
Jack Penney*
Mark Perry

HE'S DANSIN:
Norman Mercier*
Mark Perry
John Rodger
Jorge Vargas*
Verron Bush

DULY ROYAL & AGATHA C:
Rudy Baez*
Jose Caraballo*
Carol Dudley
Bill Klinke*
Henry Ma*

PENANCE:
Jennifer Jarvis
George Trenger

SUNNY REIGN:
Jose Caraballo*
Sharon Cullinane
Edna Sargent

SUNNY CRIME:
Jose Caraballo*
George Trenger

SUNNY STAND:
Maureen Blanchette
Jose Caraballo*
Dorothy Gentner
Aimee Hall
Greg Knight

DUE TO LAND:
Rudy Baez*
Maureen Blanchette*
Dorothy Gentner
Bill Klinke*
Greg Knight

DUE TO SHINE:
Ken Houghton
Gregg Knight
Chris McKenzie
Dennis Nobles
Miguel Santiago

DULY'S DANCER:
Rudy Baez*
Dennis Nobles
Harry Vega*
Rachael Walsh

REGAN'S RIDGE:
Jose Caraballo*
Jackie Falk
Jennifer Jarvis
Dennis Nobles
Jose Vargas*
Rachael Walsh

SUNDANCE LAND:
Ken Houghton
Tim Kirby

PARTY PANTS:
Chuck Patti
Rachael Walsh

Fueling the fires of all these horses: Frank and Terry Burke of Dodge Grain, purveyors of food and bedding through all the years, through all the seasons.

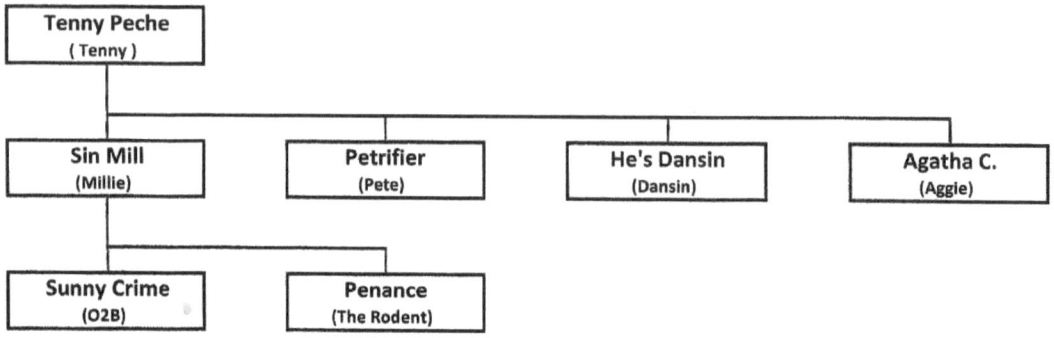

Note: Sunny Clips was the sire of Sunny Crime

Chain of Foals
Royal Stand Family Tree

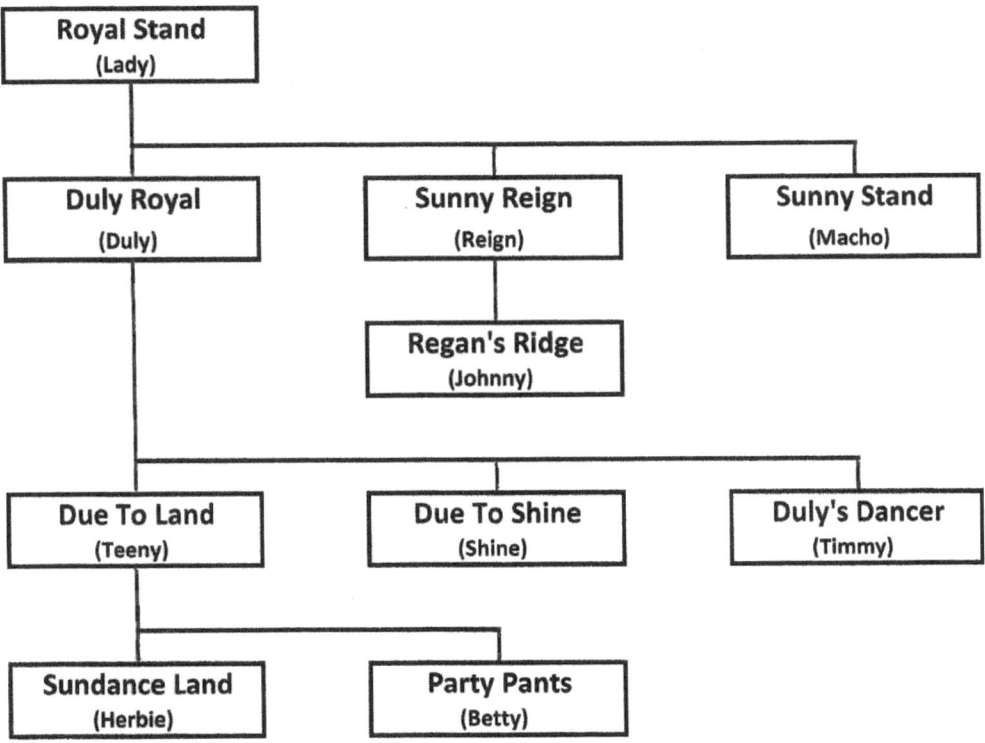

Note: Sunny Clips was the sire of Sunny Reign, Sunny Crime, Sunny Stand, and Due to Shine

Tom Schwigen, one of the greatest starters in the business, and two of our best jockeys, Joe Hampshire and Tammi Piermarini.

The Winner's Circle

We did have a pretty good run. From the birth of the first foal to the last it was a span of twenty-five years. That all our foals made it to the racetrack was pretty amazing in itself. We had horses that made it to the races but never won, and others who had brilliance. Our percentages were very good, too, which was surprising, considering that we were very naive at the outset, and never did own a farm of our own. We were smart enough, though, to realize early on that breeding every mare every year would be financially overwhelming. Working at the track was a revelation to me. I learned so much from so many wonderful people, trainers who were absolutely brilliant at bringing out the best in their horses, exercise riders who had equine ESP, grooms who could relate to their horses in amazing ways. It is a wonderful world!

When I trained our horses myself, I was fortunate to have excellent exercise riders. Having tact on horseback, being able to feel how the horse was moving, sensing where his strengths and weaknesses were-these abilities were absolutely critical to my training. I never could have achieved what I did without the riders' support and feedback. Some of my favorites: Mark Perry, Dennis Nobles, Rachael Walsh, Dorothy Gertner, Guy Henry, Henry Ma, Kenny Houghton, Maureen Blanchette, Chris McKenzie, Sharon Cullinane. Jockeys, these brave, talented people, are also essential to success on the track. I profited greatly from the ability of Tony Barreira, Vernon Bush, Jose Caraballo, Harry Vega, Billy Klinke, Rudy Baez, Brent Kelly, Henry Ma, Maureen Blanchette and Greg Knight. They not only worked with my horses in the morning, but rode them in the afternoon too. The late Norman Mercier, the incomparable Denise Boudrot, Tammy Campbell (who changed into Tammi Piermarini): it was a privilege to work with these brave, underrated athletes and consummate horsemen. I will also always cherish my friendship with Tom Schwigen, the starter. We had a rough beginning, but I realized that he was absolutely correct in insisting that a horse be relaxed in the starting gate. He was a dedicated horseman, and a wonderful human being. His gate crew was the best in the country. I feel privileged to have been considered one of his friends. Cathy Chumbley, a devoted pony person and later, the afternoon outrider, treated my horses as if they were her own, as did Robby Holman, who was my main man to get these sensitive critters to the paddock safely.

The casual reader, if he has come to this point, is probably wondering why we went on. So many times, our horses would show brilliance, and then come up with some ailment, or tease us along with flashes of talent in the morning, and then bomb out in the afternoon. Highs and lows go with every endeavor, but in horseracing, they seem more extreme. We all know, however, that there is nothing else in life more moving than seeing a horse aware of his own ability, running with grace and beauty on the racetrack, and watching a horse we've delivered ourselves come down the stretch and cross the wire in front has given us a thrill that is unequaled. Paul Mellon, in an interview in Time Magazine many years ago, expressed these thoughts, and they resonate with anyone who's ever bred and raced a Thoroughbred. Whether a millionaire or hands on breeder/trainer, the thrill is the same. We'll always have those Win pictures.

Due to Land (Teeny) and Bill Klinke get up to win at Rockingham.

The Dope on Drugs

I hear uninformed people say it all the time: "Oh, race horses all run on drugs!" Well, that may have been true in those old racing movies of the 1930's, but most racetracks today have strict procedures to ensure that horses do NOT run on drugs. First of all, the winner of every race is always sent to the test barn. Others are, too. Often the horse who finishes second, horses who have been claimed, and others chosen by the stewards. At the test barn, which is a restricted area, horses stay until they have provided the necessary samples. The samples themselves are sealed, in the presence of a state supervisor, assigned numbers, and signed off by a licensed person involved with that horse. Then, the samples are sent to an outside laboratory for testing.

When the samples are at the lab, there's nothing there involving racing, it's all chemists and their assistants. If something is detected in a sample, strict protocols are followed, and the number of the sample is given to the authorities at the track, who then notify the trainer of the horse in question.

Today, there is a long list of possible medications a horse may be given. The list is separated into classes, and the penalties for violations vary according to the class. Class 1 medication violations are the most severe: these are medications that should never find their way into a horse, and violations usually mean significant suspensions. For medications that horses may be given for a variety of reasons, there are thresholds determined, and appropriate withdrawal times. Trainers of horses who test positive are given the option of a split sample: the original sample is divided, and the part as yet untested is tested to make sure the sample was, in fact, the one it was supposed to be.

In a horse's training, there may be times when he needs medication. A cut? Antibiotic. Colic? A slight fever? Hives? There are many medications appropriate here, which is fine just as long as the medication is withdrawn far enough before a race to avoid getting a positive. It has been a long road to get to this point, where things are spelled out quite clearly. Milton Toby wrote a book about the infamous Dancer's Image Derby of 1968. He was disqualified for a Bute positive, but the methods of detection in those days were casual, at best.

Later, in 1994, one of our horses was caught up in the transition from the casual testing to the precise protocol of today. Our horse, Sunny Stand, won a race at Suffolk Downs in the spring. Then, Suffolk was quiet for the summer. On opening day in the fall, Sunny Stand ran in a stakes race and won! A wonderful moment of glory for all of us. Then, a few weeks later, I was sitting on a bucket in front of his stall while he was enjoying his whirlpool boots. It was a dark day, so there was no one else around, but he had his whirlpool treatment every day, and we were getting ready for his next race. Suddenly, a man approached us, and said to me, "Is this Sunny Stand?" Now, I didn't know this man. I'd seen him marching around the backside, in cowboy boots and a bomber jacket, but I didn't know who he was. My first thought was, "Oh, God! This is a hit man!" since my horse was the big favorite for the coming race. No, he waved a paper in front of me and said, "He got a positive test. I should toss your tack room!" Well, I was stunned. How could this happen? I knew exactly what my horse ate, and when. Well, after the man left, I called my vet and mentioned "a curious thing" that had just happened. She grew quiet, and said, "That sounds like the state cop!"

Well, it was true, Macho had tested positive for isoxsuprine. Was I giving him isoxsuprine? Absolutely, little tablets I put in his feed. His big body/flat feet conformation gave him the tendency to be footsore and this medication helped his peripheral circulation. He'd been getting it for months. He'd won in the spring when he was getting it, and he was fine. I always stopped giving the pills a week before his race, and had never had a problem.

The next day, I had to appear before the stewards, who gave me a crushing suspension and took back the purse. I had the right to appeal, so I called on a lawyer friend, and we appeared before the commission. More things came to light. Over the summer, the state chemist (at that time the state had its own lab for horse and dog tests) had read about a controversy involving D. Wayne Lukas and his fantastic filly, Flanders, who'd had a positive for, yes, isoxsuprine. The chemist, reading this, thought it would be interesting to use an ELISA test for this substance, so he got the samples from opening day, and, voila, Sunny Stand had a flag for that drug, indicating exposure. The chemist did further treatment of the sample, did more tests, and got the positive. Well, at that time, the commission had not practiced today's rules: there were no split samples, and there was no quantifying. The ELISA test showed isoxsuprine had been in the horse in the past, but not when, and not how much. The commission hearing was actually quite interesting, or would have been had it not been me and my horse that they were talking about. I was frozen to the chair.

Since this story involved opening day, a stakes race, and the chairman of the Massachusetts Thoroughbred Breeders (me!) the papers went wild. Big headlines appeared in both Boston papers, including a hideous file photo of me smiling insanely. It was horrifying. I was still teaching and one of my colleagues leaned over at lunch one day and said, "Oh, I read the Globe, but I told my husband, 'Oh, Susan would never drug her horse!'" Mortifying was an understatement. To their credit, both the writers for the Globe and the Herald went out of their way to be fair. Ed Gray zeroed in on the lack of quantifying test samples, saying there was no way to tell if the drug was "a memory, or running out the horses' nose."

When the dust had settled (and when my hair had gone completely white), the commission did take away Macho's purse, but they held me blameless, which was unprecedented. Shortly after that, a committee was formed to discuss testing methods. I was on the committee, and we visited the state lab to watch their procedures. There I got to meet the chemist, who later became a friend. The focus on the methodology did yield positive results: now there are split samples, and now there is quantifying. The list of acceptable medications is lengthy, and includes withdrawal times for all, so it is difficult to get a positive test "by accident." Positives do occur, though, but with the right to appeal, and with split samples and quantifying, the whole process is much more scientific. For me, back in 1994, however; it was a nightmare!

Robby and Greg taking Teeny to the paddock at Rockingham:
It takes a village!

Some Random Conclusions

I. I really feel that a mare should foal with minimum supervision: no foaling parties, group pictures, lights camera action! The mares who've had a foal try very hard with subsequent ones to go into labor when we're not looking, so I try to respect that.

II. If we expect to send our foals to a racetrack and have a career there, it helps to expose them to many different people's handling. We try to make sure that the people who break them are the best. This doesn't have to mean the most expensive or most famous, just people who are in this for the genuine love of horses.

III. We had three horses come up with tendons in training. When Shine's tendon started bothering her, we tried constant monitoring, ultrasounds frequently, control over her exercise, and in spite of all that hovering, she never made it to the races. When Teeny bowed, she had already had knee surgery, was tough to train calmly, and difficult to manage, so we just brought her home and let her go right out to the pasture. She raced around for a day or so, and then settled down. Today, I can't remember which leg the bow was on. Nature made it go away! When Timmy's tendon surfaced, we were devastated, of course, and when he went home, I turned him out at first in a small paddock, and wrapped it. Eleven months after the initial bow, I thought it was almost gone; and if we'd planned to keep him going, I'd probably have put him back in training. We didn't, so I let him keep on, and by twelve months and two weeks, it was completely gone. Tendons take time. Period.

IV. There is a statistic somewhere that shows that a majority of major stakes winners are homebreds. I can see why. When we bred a horse, we didn't have the luxury of going to a sales and scrutinizing every inch. We had to take what we were given, and sometimes, we were pleasantly surprised. Conversely, our biggest duds, and disappointments, had nothing physical to indicate that.

V. The most important people in our quest were our exercise riders. They were absolutely crucial to a horse's training. Good exercise riders taught the horse to love going to the track in the morning, to use his body efficiently, to relax coming back, to look forward to the next day under saddle. Their feedback to us was critical in our understanding of how our horses were doing, how fit they were, what the potential problems were.

VI. Whoever said, "A bad day at the racetrack is still better than a good day any place else," was absolutely correct.

VII. My racetrack life played out at Rockingham Park and Suffolk Downs. Rockingham is now history, and Suffolk is on the endangered-species list, but it will always have a place in my heart. Mention Suffolk Downs, or post a picture on Facebook, and you'll get an immediate response. It has a long history and a huge devoted family.

Sin Mill at Rockingham when she was a 2 year old. She's in John Burke's barn, and Jeff Rosen is holding her while Joey Prince looks on.

Sunny Reign breaks from the gate for her second win.

CHAIN OF FOALS

EPILOGUE

Duly Royal and her first foal, Due to Land.

Chain of Foals

I started writing this to document our attempts at raising race horses, but I realized that my experiences also provide a glimpse into the last years of horse racing in New England. My account covers the years from 1975 to 2010. In the seventies, there were small fair meets in the area, two tracks in Rhode Island, one in Vermont, and Rockingham and Suffolk both had significant racing. Now, the fairs and the Rhode Island tracks are history, Rockingham has been closed for years, and in 2015 began to disappear. All of the racing paraphernalia was auctioned off in 2016, and at this writing, everything has been demolished. Suffolk closed for good in 2019, so this wonderful sport will soon be just a memory for us in New England too.

When I was young, I went to Rockingham with my mother and older sister once to see the races (September 1, 1958). I spent most of the time looking over my shoulder, afraid of being ousted for being underage, but we stood at trackside and watched the races unfurl, and my older sister even placed a bet for me on a horse named In the Country, who led the whole way until the eighth pole. I loved the sport, but thought it was something to observe, not to participate in. I contented myself by making a scrapbook of all the racing coverage in Sports Illustrated. Years later, in the seventies, when I met John Roche and realized that local people could actually be a part of all this, I was stunned. My next actual appearance at the track was one day when I took one of John's horses to Suffolk Downs for him. His daughter, Cathy, went with me. She was too young to be a trainer, so Ned Allard saddled the horse for her. It was my first trip to the backside. I carefully planned what to wear, aiming for something that would make me look as if I belonged: jeans and my riding boots. Ned's assistant was John Burke, and years later when I worked for him, he often kidded about meeting me for the first time "in those boots." I did not blend! Everything was new to me, of course and the horse, Gay Charlie, won! That meant we went to the spit box (which I learned was race track vernacular for the test barn). Well, he took forever in there, and finally they sent him back to the barn with a state policeman to see if he'd give a sample there. It was then very late, and getting dark, and I heard the announcement, "All women off the backside!" which horrified me. The state cop told us we could stay, and they sent me to the track kitchen to get coffee for everyone. I walked up the alley between barns in the dark and pushed open the door to a wall of noise, and a solid crowd of men, all standing around in the smoke and gloom. It was all so strange to me, and scary, but I got the coffees, returned to the barn, and the horse had cooperated in the meantime. It was a long, exciting day I'll never forget.

A few years later, when our first foal was born, I decided to spend my summer vacation working at Rockingham and I secured a job as hot walker. From the first day, I fell in love with life on the backside. The fact that I was already married, with horses at home, probably saved me from running away to join the racetrack circus.

Rockingham in the seventies was a wonderful place. People there were very competitive, of course; but also very kind. Horse racing has no place for airs. A horse's breeding, an owner's budget, the quality of your tack-once the gates open, none of that matters. The people on the backside don't pass judgment on you; they treat people with college degrees the same as high school dropouts. What matters there is how good you are at what you do. When I arrived for my hot walker job, I knew nothing about the backstretch. Yes, my trusty horse was an ex-racehorse, but the whole culture was foreign to me. I was not a kid, I didn't come from a race track family, my two degrees and a steady job as a Latin teacher were completely irrelevant, but I never, even on that first day, felt unwelcome or out of place. Everyone was friendly, everyone was helpful.

The first few summers I worked at Rockingham, most of the trainers were men, as were most of the jockeys. Most of the grooms were young boys and college girls home for the summer. There were some black grooms from the south, too, second and third generation professional horsemen. Over the years, Hispanics became more and more prevalent, until in my last few years as a trainer, I often spoke as much Spanish in the morning as English. Gradually, more and more women joined the ranks of trainers and exercise riders. Now, women trainers are common; but I don't see the "girls-on-summer-vacation" grooms the way I used to. Few of the grooms from the seventies saw their children follow in their shoes. A huge percentage of the backstretch help now is Hispanic. In the seventies, Denise Boudrot, through her obvious skill, dispelled the old prejudices against women riders, so more and more women became jockeys. Now, jockeys like Tammi Piermarini prove on a daily basis that this is a field where women can compete with men. Again, on the backstretch, what matters is your ability, not your race, sex, or tax bracket. As my mentor John Burke used to say, the track is "the last bastion of democracy."

Rockingham was the perfect track for summer. There were lakes close by, where many trainers rented vacation homes. The backside was roomy, there were pockets of grass where you could hand graze a horse or have a leisurely lunch. The track kitchen was inviting, and the public had access. Long lines of racing fans would form there before the first race, and they could sit at a table and inhale the racetrack atmosphere. In my memory, it was always sunny. The track kitchen always had its windows wide open, and gentle breezes would blow through. I could order chicken wings with blue cheese dressing and watch the races from Saratoga with my friends. The paddock was inside the grandstand, so we'd walk the horses up the length of the stretch, up the ramp between the clubhouse and grandstand, and inside to the paddock. There were trainers who came for the summer with enough horses to fill a whole barn. They'd have the same barn for years. There was a small track way out back, across a back road, "Nutters," where you could just pony a horse or gallop quietly, without the intense training on the main track. There was a field behind the grandstand where teams played softball, and behind the track kitchen, there were sometimes real fights, with a makeshift ring and lots of cheering onlookers. There was a small chapel, where Chaplain Lee held regular services; there was a day-care center where the backstretch children could play while their parents worked. Next to the kitchen was a small building which held Waldeck's tack shop, with an old wooden porch. Life was relaxed, life was good.

In 1980, on a beautiful summer morning, a fire started in the wooden grandstand during training hours. Within minutes, it spread to the whole structure, and changed life forever at this track. The wind that day was blowing across the infield and down across the back field, and fortunately that kept the smoke and debris from the stable area. People stood around in groups at the gap and watched as the firemen battled the flames, knowing that life at this New Hampshire track would never be the same. That is a day I'll never forget. Because of the way the wind was blowing, the sound of the fire didn't carry. People just stood and watched. I remember the silence: no one talked or commented. We just stood around silently as our whole world changed in front of our eyes.

That fire marked the end of Rockingham as we knew it. Obviously, without a grandstand, racing could not continue. Suffolk Downs scrambled around and opened sooner than planned, so most people moved there for the rest of the season, but Rockingham was closed for four long years. Finally, with a new, smaller grandstand, it reopened in 1984. The backstretch was essentially the same, but the Rockingham Mall replaced the field behind the grandstand. There was no more softball field, no more sawmill barn in the hinterlands. The new grandstand had an outside paddock between it and the old administration building, with a small building for the jockeys. Some of the big outfits that used to summer there had in the interim made other plans and the people who took their place had fewer horses. Now, it was unusual for a whole barn to be occupied by one outfit.

Suffolk, meanwhile, having had a monopoly on racing for four years, wasn't ready to give up the nice summer months, so for a while, both tracks ran at the same time. All the usual suspects who had moved from Rockingham were still at Suffolk, so the "new" Rockingham was filled for the most part by a whole fresh crop of trainers and their retinues.

Now racing in the summer, Suffolk had become a year-round track. Being right in the city, the stable area was laid out efficiently, with barns in two rows along a main road, and in the winter the maintenance people did a fantastic job plowing snow and keeping the access to the horses safe. There must be a special place in heaven for people who raced in New England in the winter. Even though the crews did their best, working with the horses in the snow and cold was brutal. I remember many times having to carry water buckets to the ladies' room to thaw them out and refill them. The track staff put plastic sheets up along the open sides of the barns, to keep out the cold, and on windy days, they would snap like whips. There were no days off for the people who took care of the horses, either. One day in particular, it was snowing heavily, and I set out from my home in North Andover in my ancient Chevy station wagon. I reasoned that it was downhill all the way, so I motored on and when I got to Route 1, it hadn't been plowed yet. Still, the Chevy soldiered on. This was before four-wheel drive, too! As I lumbered through the drifts, I noticed that there was an ancient boat of a Cadillac in front of me. It was John Roger, coming in from the Roche farm in Haverhill. When I finally made it to the track and staggered to the kitchen to revive, it was packed with people all in a good mood, all hyped from having made it in safely. They managed to keep the track open for training all winter, too, even though the horses would often come off the track with whiskers lined in ice. Racing went on.

In 1981, a few breeders got together and formed the Massachusetts Thoroughbred Breeders' Association. I was one of the original board members, but all the credit for structuring the association and getting it passed into legislation belongs to Linda Powell. She had the vision and energy to get us up to Beacon Hill and plead our cause. It was a great program, funded by a percentage of the handle at the track and providing bonuses to owners, breeders and stallion owners. Linda had the drive to ensure we had an executive director, too, one who understood the workings of politics. Her future husband, Gordon Ramsey, was the first, then Mark Regan, and Dave Hollway. These three gentlemen ensured that every time a racing bill came before the state, the breeders would improve their position. We started putting on stakes races for Massbreds, too, and even had a yearling show at the track for the first few years. Under Linda's leadership, the foal crop grew to over two hundred, and the quality of the Massbreds improved considerably. Soon, it was not unusual for Massbreds to distinguish themselves in open company. This would never have happened without Linda's guidance. Most of the rest of us were horse people who had no idea who the key legislators were, or how to produce a viable piece of legislation. My main contribution? I designed and drew our logo. Here's a piece of trivia: both the foal and the outline of the racehorse in the logo are our first foal, Sin Mill. A Massbred, of course!

Rockingham's disaster of a fire was in 1980. New England racing had a few peaceful years, and then in 1989 it was Suffolk's turn to be in crisis. The owner of the track announced in the fall that he was closing. Naturally, all the people who'd struggled to keep racing alive were devastated. As fall turned to winter, the days got colder, and the owner announced that, since he was closing at the end of December, he wouldn't winterize the track. Still, racing went on. Everyone was more determined than ever to keep going, even when the cold weather turned the track to freeze-dried powder. We ran one of our horses that year just before it closed. It was a frigid day, and there were dust storms like talcum powder. Still, no one wanted to scratch and no jockeys whined about quitting. That day, our horse won, and we were ecstatic, of course. Then, the Racing Commissioner himself showed up, to make sure everyone was able to function in these adverse conditions and we convinced him to be in the winner's circle with us.

A few days later, it was over. Some of the trainers at Suffolk were going south for the winter, of course, but for many locals, the only choice was Rockingham, which was generous in providing stalls. I may have been one of the last to leave. I remember driving down the main road in my station wagon, all my traps, the buckets, the stall guards, the tack, the bandages, piled in back, and slowing down as I passed the gate. I was sure that someone was going to stop me, someone would jump out and say, "Wait! Go back! We're staying open!" but there was no one there except for the regular guard, who waved a sad goodbye as I drove out.

When I got to Rockingham, even though I had fond memories of summers there, it was like a foreign country. I ended up in a barn where I was the only Suffolk arrival: everyone else there was a stranger. Settling into a new barn in the dead of winter surrounded by people I didn't know was daunting, to say the least. By spring, I was more comfortable, but it was not an easy transition for any of us.

Suffolk stayed closed for two full years. Just when we thought it would never reopen, Jim Moseley and some partners bought it, and on January 1, 1992, we were back in action. That day was bright and sunny, and even warm for January. I remember being stunned at the number of cars. The whole parking lot was full, and cars lined the road all the way down past the stable area. The mood was electric and both Boston papers gave good coverage.

Jim Moseley brought new enthusiasm and style to the old place. He had the facade of the clubhouse restored to its art deco self, the inside of the whole building was gleaming, and the mood was upbeat. He restored the running of the MassCap, too and his racing staff, led by John Morrissey as the racing secretary, attracted horses that were nationally known. I'll never forget watching the great Cigar win the first two MassCaps under the Moseley regime, pulling into the barn area, escorted by the state police, walking off his van at the loading ramp greeted by a cheering crowd, including Mrs. Moseley herself, with a little camera, cheering like a schoolgirl. Then, the Paulsens arriving for the race in a helicopter, landing glamorously in the infield. When Cigar won the first time, I was sitting up in the grandstand looking down at the winner's circle. The whole circle was crammed with people. Cigar waded into their midst, his handsome, sweaty head raised above the crowd, and then a bejeweled, manicured hand reached up from the sea of people to pat his gritty neck: Madeleine Paulsen herself!

Those years were wonderful. Suffolk had always had a great feeling of camaraderie, and now, with Jim Moseley's leadership, they had genuine pride in the track itself. Local horses were profiting from the generous Massbred program, and no one was referring to it as "Sufferin' Downs" anymore! Rockingham was not doing as well, and finally in 2002 they raced Standardbreds only. Then, the charismatic Jim Moseley passed away. The remaining owners sold Suffolk in 2007, and under new ownership, things were fine, for a while. They revived the Massachusetts Handicap, did a lot of community outreach, and made plans for a casino. In 2014 the Gaming Commission awarded the casino license-but to someone else! The track owners decided at once that they did not want to continue, and planned to close the facility. People prevailed upon them to offer "boutique" meets: three days in 2015, three weekends in 2016, 2017, 2018 and 2019. This was all done on a ship and run basis. There was no long-term stabling, and food and drinks were provided on race days only by food trucks. Still, the loyalty people felt for the venerable old track was touching: those days were lively and upbeat: ten thousand or so fans showed up, and the fields were all full.

Now, once again, Suffolk has been sold. This time, the new owners have other plans for the property and now the end of racing in New England is in sight.

Racing in New England was far, far more meaningful to those who participated than simply a rundown of track ownership, though. It was very much a family sport. Horsemen like JJ Kelly, Lloyd Lockhart, John Kirby and Peter Petro raised their kids on the backside, kids who went on to be trainers themselves, or jockeys, and even the grandkids, too. Even today, post one old picture of the backside on Facebook, and you can expect a flurry of hits and comments. Racing was hard work, of course, physical work, but it was also full of laughter. Most of my memories involve friends laughing about something. Political correctness did not have a foothold on the backstretch. There were nicknames, usually mocking someone's physical appearance. You could know someone really well, share experiences for years, and yet you didn't know his real name. The track kitchen was a refuge from bad weather, a break from work. The food was good, and nourishing. At Suffolk, I remember watching Cigar win the very first World Cup, standing in a huge crowd of people in the track kitchen, elbow to elbow, eyes riveted on the television. There was always a card game going on in the Rec Hall, too. One year, I set up a simple rack and filled it with paperbacks, "free to a good home." I was encouraged to see how fast the books disappeared, but I soon realized that, for every one taken to read, there was another used to pack horses' feet, or keep score in the card games. There was an observation room at the gap at Suffolk, where you could watch the horses train in bad weather, and that was always a source of news and gossip. I remember standing at the rail in the morning, talking to the outriders, Paul Cimini at first, then Kathy Chumbley, and John Manning at Rockingham.

Then, there are the goats. I remember Sheryl Meade's goat Shirley, who loved to stand on the porch of the track kitchen at Suffolk and challenge everyone walking in. We had a goat too: Jerry, who was inseparable from one of our horses. Then, there was Rudi, a huge dark brown goat owned by

Paulette Secretant. One day Paulette came to me in tears. Rudi had gone for days without "passing fluids." She was sure he would die or blow up! I made a quick call to my dog's vet, Dr. Prentiss, and he agreed to look at him. We loaded him in the back seat of my trusty Chevy station wagon, and I headed to North Andover. At every red light, someone would yell out a crack about my "ugly husband" and when I rolled up the window, the air inside reeked of "eau de goat." When we arrived at Dr. Prentiss' vet hospital, I led Rudi into the waiting room, an immaculate area with framed pictures of kittens and puppies. When he beckoned Rudi into the examining room, the stress of the trip and the relief of being out of the car triggered a release, a release of goat urine that flooded the room along with a toxic cloud of goat aroma. A few years later, I drove over with my dog for a routine visit, and there was a goat outside. Dr. Prentiss yelled over, "You'll note that we do goat exams outside now!"

Our barns were our "home away from home." The track tended to assign us the same barn every year, so we got really entrenched. Unless we had enough horses to fill the whole barn, we had no control over the other occupants; so we learned quickly how to coexist with a variety of personalities. Getting along with others was another life lesson learned at the racetrack.

Why do we feel so strongly about these memories? Perhaps it has a lot to do with the adversity. It is physically grueling to work on the backside, and dangerous, too. I will never forget the day jockeys Vinnie Amico and Rudy Baez went down at Rockingham, and Gary Donohue and Mike Lapensee at Suffolk. Their lives changed forever in seconds. It was not dangerous just on the track, either. I remember a friend who had a horse plant his hoof on his skull when he was putting bandages on him, and another young boy kicked in the head standing outside his barn. I myself got an outstanding black eye from one of my own horses, and have long since stopped keeping track of all the bites. One summer, we took a few days' vacation to Saratoga, and Jim took a picture of me sitting on the terrace at the Gideon Putnam. My hair was actually more or less combed, I was neatly dressed, and I was smiling discreetly-and on my left arm? An enormous purple, black and blue "rose," a parting gift from my horse. With the ever present risk of injury to both horse and human, the focus had to be on humor, on the satisfaction of washing a horse down after a brilliant work, and the fabulous euphoria in the winner's circle.

The common denominator for all of us, of course, is the horse. Horses keep us honest. In racing, a horse's ability is the only thing that counts. Pedigree, appearance, horse clothing, horse owners, all of these are nice but meaningless. Ability wins the races. The people, therefore, can't take on airs. There are no snobs on the backside, since a good horse can pop up anywhere. Our humble homebreds have beaten horses bought as yearlings for fortunes. We once won a race with a first time starter who beat the heavy favorite. His owner owned the track, too! Horses are fragile: today's winner may be retired tomorrow. A hard-knocking horse of yours may be claimed and end up in another barn the next time he runs. The good times are fleeting, the future is uncertain, so we have to get along, we have to enjoy a nice sunny afternoon, or a particularly beautiful gallop, or the gleam of a dappled-out coat. We have to focus on the good times, the funny stories, and the unforgettable people. When two track people meet up after a few years, the stories start: "Remember when Dave was riding that little bay" or "Remember that crazy stall walker who…" The memories float up to the surface; the past is revived.

The winner of the Kentucky Derby in 2017 was Always Dreaming. This would be a great motto for a horseman at the track: that's what we are! Doing stalls, cleaning the tack, picking the feet, we always hope that this one will be "The One." All of us are always dreaming.

Good times at the track!
With Jose Caraballo and Cathy Chumbley.

Photo Credits

Ellen Alden: 196

Liisa Jackson: 245

Leesa Lavigne: 118

Mary Pitt: 138, 189, 200, 242, 243, 254, 264, 275

Chris Robey: 215

Sara Taylor: 244